Stories I
Need to Tell

Vol. 1

SCREENPLAYS BY DOUGLAS KING

DAY
III
Productions
film • publishing • events

ISBN: 978-1-7350083-2-5

www.DayIIIProd.com

DAY
III
Productions
film • publishing • events

INTRODUCTION

I have been writing screenplays professionally for three decades. In that time, I have written scripts I am immensely proud of, and others that, well, let's just say, the fact they never saw the silver screen is probably a good thing for all parties concerned. I have written for major studios, independent studios, independent producers as well as my own spec scripts, some of which you hold in our hands now.

Screenplays by their very essence are just stories presented in a format that makes them accessible for other creative individuals (directors, costume designers, set designers and actors, to name a few) to produce a motion picture or television show. As most writers know, getting a spec screenplay sold and produced into a film is tantamount to winning the lottery. The odds may actually be better to win the lottery.

In light of this, and despite this, I have continued to write my screenplays for many reasons. First, I truly love the process and enjoy breaking story, developing character and plot and working out the story beats. Second, call me delusional, but there is an optimistic part of me that still believes these scripts may be sold and produced one day, which ultimately leads me to my final reason for what some might say is a sadomasochistic endeavor, I must tell these stories.

These stories, characters, settings and themes have burrowed themselves so deeply into my mind and psyche that if I do not release them onto the page, like a geothermal geyser, they would simply burst forth through the mantel of my mind causing who knows what type of irreparable damage.

What you hold in your hands is the product of many years of writing. Each volume in this series includes two spec screenplays of stories I have to tell. It has become a moral imperative that I release these stories to the public. And, if they are not made into the films they are meant to mature into, transitioning from a caterpillar to a beautiful butterfly, then at least they can be enjoyed in their pupa form within the pages of this book.

I hope you enjoy these stories. If you do and if you would like to see them metamorphosize into what they can be—a life action feature film—let me know. The best by-product of screenwriting is that it blooms into the collaborative art of filmmaking and storytelling.

These are the stories I need to tell. Maybe we can tell some together.

In this first volume you will find two screenplays with the theme of female empowerment. Since having a daughter, my eyes have been opened to the various trials and tribulations that woman still must face in this so-called modern age. Society continues to place stereotypes and labels on young women even though we have been calling for change for centuries.

The story of Esther goes back to the B.C. period of the Old Testament and tells the saga of a strong, young woman who shoulders the fate and burden of the entire Jewish nation upon her shoulders. While *Esther* is the story of one historical woman, *Top Five* is the story of two young women making history through a pageant scholarship program. The very word "pageant" generates stereotypes and stigmas. From my first-hand experience with the Miss America organization, I can tell you, the intangible benefits young women who participate in this close-knit sorority gain, are far greater than any stereotypical perceptions.

Both stories deal with preconceived notions, prejudice, hatred (in its many forms), but also acceptance, love and sisterhood. These are stories I knew I had to tell in support, encouragement and inspiration for my own daughter but also, all young women. The fact is, I must tell these stories because my daughter has inspired me, and I simply want to return the favor.

Douglas King
February 2020

LOGLINE

During the rule of King Ahasuerus, a young Jewish girl is placed in life or death peril when she must hide her true nationality from the king and members of his court bent on destroying all Jews, when she is selected to be the queen.

Esther
A Night of Destiny

by
Douglas King

Adapted from the book of Esther from the Old Testament

FADE IN

EXT. PERSIAN DESERT - DUSK

The sun is setting on the hot Persian desert. The capital
city of Shushan is backlit and glowing in the setting sun.

TEXT FADES IN OVER THE SCENE. THE TEXT BEGINS IN HEBREW
LETTERS AND TRANSFORMS TO ENGLISH.

"In the year 483 BC, King Ahasuerus -- known as Xerxes to the
Greeks -- reigned over one hundred and twenty-seven
provinces, from India to Ethiopia, and set his throne in
Shushan (Susa) the citadel.

"The Hebrews lived in Persia having been brought there in
captivity by Nebuchadnezzar, King of Babylon, and were hated
by many in the land."

INT. ROYAL HALL - NIGHT

KING AHASUERUS is overseeing his seven day feast for the
people of Shushan. The king is a tall, good looking man. Long
dark hair frames his olive complexion face and dark eyes.

A great hall is lavishly decorated and throngs of people are
eating, drinking, and being merry. MUSIC is playing and
ENTERTAINERS perform for the GUESTS.

Finely dressed SERVANTS pour wine to the guests in golden
vessels, each vessel being different from the other.

CONCUBINES fill the hall and are intermingling with the men.

King Ahasuerus is enjoying the entire affair and drinking
deeply of wine. He is drunk and merry.

Sitting with the king are princes from the many provinces of
his land, these are his wise men, and counsel, CARSHENA,
SHETHAR, ADMATHA, TARASHISH, MERES, MARSENA, and MEMUCAN.

King Ahasuerus stops his drinking to look out over the sea of
people enjoying his feast.

He calls for HATHACH one of his eunuchs. Hathach is a bear of
a man. Dark skinned and powerfully muscular.

                    KING AHASUERUS
          I wish to display the queen for all
          of my guests.
                    (MORE)

                    KING AHASUERUS (CONT'D)
          Have her come at once attired in
          her best robes and the royal crown
          so that my guests may look upon her
          beauty. She is without doubt the
          most lovely woman in all the land
          and certainly this hall tonight.

                    HATHACH
          Yes, my lord. As you command.

Hathach gathers six other EUNUCHS and they leave to fetch the
Queen.

INT. QUEEN VASHTI'S HALL - NIGHT

QUEEN VASHTI is also hosting a feast in her own royal hall.
This feast is more subdued but no less lavish in its
decoration or the banquet before the all FEMALE GUESTS.

Eunuchs line the walls watching over the Queen and the other
women.

The Queen is beautiful. In her late thirties. She is dressed
in the finest clothes and her hair and makeup are perfect to
the last detail.

She is laughing and enjoying the feast.

Hathach enters the hall and is respectful before the Queen as
he approaches.

                    HATHACH
          My Queen, the King has summoned you
          to his feast. It is his desire that
          you should be seen by his guests in
          your best robes and wearing the
          royal crown.

                    QUEEN VASHTI
          What he desires is to parade me
          like one of his harem girls before
          the drunken masses.

                    HATHACH
          This is not a request my Queen.

                    QUEEN VASHTI
          Do not forget to whom you speak. My
          father is one of the seven most
          noble and ancient families in this
          region. Tell the king I cannot
          leave my own feast at this time, as
          it would be rude.

                    HATHACH
        As you wish.

Hathach and his six eunuchs leave the Queen's hall.

INT. ROYAL HALL - NIGHT

The feast is still raging and King Ahasuerus seems pleased
with the evening.

Hathach and the other eunuchs enter the hall and wait for the
King's approval to approach him.

                    KING AHASUERUS
        Where is my queen? Is she near?

                    HATHACH
        I am sorry my lord. The queen has
        refused to come at the king's
        command.

King Ahasuerus stands and SHOUTS.

                    KING AHASUERUS
        What? On what basis has the queen
        refused me? Is she ill?

                    HATHACH
        No my lord. She is hosting a feast
        of her own and she fears it would
        be rude to leave her guests.

Ahasuerus turns to his wise counsel of princes.

                    KING AHASUERUS
        And what of my guests? Is her
        reproach to them to be overlooked?

The princes look to each other for answers. Vizier HAMAN is
the first to respond to the King.

Haman is a devious looking man, dark and cunning. His speech
is smooth and well thought-out. Haman is not well liked by
the other princes.

                    HAMAN
        It displeases your princes to see
        you in such torment during your
        most spectacular feast.

                    KING AHASUERUS
        Thanks be to you Haman for your
        concern on my behalf.

MEMUCAN steps forward to respond. Memucan is a slight man,
but powerful in speech and <u>respected by his peers</u>.

> MEMUCAN
> Queen Vashti has not only wronged
> the king, but also all the princes,
> and all the people who are in all
> the provinces of King Ahasuerus.
> For the queen's behavior will
> become known to all women, so that
> they will despise their husbands in
> their eyes. This very day the noble
> ladies of Persia and Media will say
> to all the king's officials that
> they have heard of the behavior of
> the queen. Thus there will be
> excessive contempt and wrath. If it
> pleases the king, let a royal
> decree go out from him, and let it
> be recorded in the laws of the
> Persians and the Medes, so that it
> will not be altered, that Vashti
> shall come no more before King
> Ahasuerus; and let the king give
> her royal position to another who
> is better than she. When the king's
> decree which he will make, is
> proclaimed throughout all his
> empire (for it is great), all wives
> will honor their husbands, both
> great and small.

The other princes nod their approval of Memucan's response.

> HAMAN
> It is good what Memucan has said.
> My King do not be troubled by this
> offense tonight. State your decree
> and come, let us return to your
> feast, where we can resume the
> drinking and enjoy the
> entertainment.

> KING AHASUERUS
> Maybe you are right. Let it be
> known through-out my kingdom, in
> each province's own script and
> every people's own language.

> HAMAN
> It would do the King good to put
> away the memories of Vashti now. I
> am sure there are many a concubine
> that will help the king to do this.

The princes laugh in agreement.

EXT. SHUSHAN CITADEL - MORNING

A new day is dawning on King Ashasuerus' kingdom.

It is quiet and dark clouds are rolling through the sky.
THUNDER can be heard in the distance.

INT. QUEEN VASHTI'S CHAMBERS - MORNING

Queen Vashti is rising for the morning.

Her MAID SERVANTS are gathering for her an outfit to be
dressed in.

Suddenly the doors to her chamber burst open and the KING'S
GUARD forcibly enter the room, pushing aside the EUNUCHS that
are standing guard in the room.

                QUEEN VASHTI
        What is the meaning of this?

                ROYAL GUARD
        By royal decree, you, Vashti, are
        here by stripped of your crown and
        title and have been banished from
        ever entering the presence of the
        king.

                QUEEN VASHTI
        What?

                ROYAL GUARD
        It is so by ordered that you must
        leave the citadel at once.

                QUEEN VASHTI
        I most assuredly will not!

Vashti attempts to move past the guards and leave the room,
but they stop her.

Her maids have all fled to the corners of the room.

                QUEEN VASHTI
        I will speak to the king! My
        husband.

                         ROYAL GUARD
               He will not take audience with you.
               If you go before him without having
               been called, you will die.

Vashti struggles with the guards, but realizes her attempts
are futile and resigns herself to her fate.

She falls to the floor crying.

EXT. SHUSHAN CITADEL - DAY

A caravan holding Vashti is exiting the citadel.

The streets are quiet as the procession slowly makes its way
out of the city.

The people respectfully move aside and bow as the covered
sedan carrying Vashti passes by.

When the ROYAL GUARDS see people bowing they stop them and
force them to stand.

EXT. BALCONY OF THE KING'S CHAMBERS - DAY

Ahasuerus stands on one of the large balcony's outside of his
personal chamber.

He looks forlorn as he stares down at the procession leaving
the citadel.

In frustration, he turns and enters his chambers.

EXT. KING'S GATE - DAY

The procession is passing the front gates to the citadel and
is about to exit the front gates.

Sitting near the gates are MORDECAI and THE SANHEDRIN. They
quietly watch as the procession passes.

Mordecai is a squat, thick man. He dresses is local clothes
rather than traditional Jewish garb. He has a full grey beard
which complements his full voice, a voice that always speaks
with authority.

The Sanhedrin are a group of nervous looking Jewish religious
elder. They each dress alike. They are older men, wise, and
thoughtful.

EXT. SHUSHAN - DAY

The caravan has left the city walls and is out in the barren land surrounding the citadel.

It continues on, leaving a dusty cloud in its wake.

The first drops of rain begin to dampen the dust.

The rain increases and soon the caravan is hidden in the downpour.

INT. THE THRONE ROOM - DAY

The king sits alone in the huge throne room.

One of his attendants approaches him, but he waves him away without a word.

EXT. SHUSHAN CITADEL - NIGHT

The rain clouds from the morning are passing in front of the moon.

EXT. BALCONY OF THE KING'S CHAMBERS - NIGHT

The king is once again on his balcony looking out into the desert in the direction in which the Vashti's caravan left.

                              FADE TO BLACK.

EXT. SHUSHAN CITEDAL - MORNING

The streets of Shushan are bustling with activity and people are opening their shops and going about their business for the day.

TEXT FADES IN OVER THE SCENE -- "THREE MONTHS LATER"

INT. THE KING'S CHAMBERS - MORNING

One of the king's ATTENDANTS enters the king's chambers to find him still in his sleeping clothes and hunched over at the edge of his bed.

                         ATTENDANT
              My king, is everything all right?

                              KING AHASUERUS
              I am alone.

                              ATTENDANT
              Do you wish that I should call one
              of your concubine?

                              KING AHASUERUS
              No. I long for the beauty of my
              lost wife, Vashti. The days were
              never as long as they are now, when
              she was near.

                              ATTENDANT
              I am sorry my king.

                              KING AHASUERUS
              Cancel whatever was planned for me
              this day. I do not wish to see
              anyone.

                              ATTENDANT
              Yes, my king.

The attendant leaves the room, leaving the king alone once
again.

INT. HALL OUTSIDE OF THE KING'S CHAMBERS - MORNING

The attendant exits the king's chambers and turns to find
himself standing face to face with Haman. Haman is dressed in
his normal black, from head to toe.

The attendant is startled by Haman's presence outside of the
king's chamber.

                              HAMAN
              Is the king ill?

                              ATTENDANT
              No. I assure you he is fine.

                              HAMAN
              Then I shall see him.

The attendant stands in Haman's way of entering the chambers.

                              ATTENDANT
              The king has asked to be left alone
              again today. He does not wish to
              see anyone.

                    HAMAN
What is this melancholy that has
bewitched the king?

                    ATTENDANT
I believe he misses the queen.

                    HAMAN
Does he not have hundreds of women
in his harem? Does not one please
him?

                    ATTENDANT
I don't know how to answer that.

                    HAMAN
I do. Let me pass and I shall
advise the king.

                    ATTENDANT
I cannot do so.

Frustrated Haman stares at the attendant. If looks could
kill, then this attendant would be long dead.

                    HAMAN
Fine. Then here is a message I wish
you to deliver for me.

INT. THE KING'S CHAMBERS - LATER - DAY

The king is dressed but still sits alone in his chambers. He
sits at a desk reading from the chronicles which describe his
every move.

His attendant enters the room and approaches the king.

                    ATTENDANT
My king. How do you feel?

                  KING AHASUERUS
Much the same.

                    ATTENDANT
If I may speak...

Not looking up from the chronicles, Ahasuerus waves his hands
in acknowledgement and gives his permission to speak.

                    ATTENDANT
          My king, it has been suggested, let
          the king appoint officers in all
          the provinces of his kingdom, that
          they may gather all the beautiful
          young virgins to Susa the citadel,
          into the women's quarters, under
          the custody of HEGAI the custodian
          of the women. And let beauty
          preparations be given them. Then
          let the young woman who pleases the
          king be queen instead of Vashti.

Ahasuerus, does not look up from his reading or react at
first.

The attendant is not sure if he was heard. He waits though so
as not to stir the king's wrath.

Slowly Ahasuerus lowers the chronicles he is reading and
places his hands on the desk. He contemplates what the
attendant has spoken.

Finally he stands and faces the attendant.

                    KING AHASUERUS
          This is good. Let it be done.

                    ATTENDANT
          As you wish my king.

The attendant backs out of the room while Ahasuerus walks to
his balcony.

EXT. BALCONY OF THE KING'S CHAMBERS - DAY

The King looks down on his city.

EXT. SHUSHAN CITEDAL - DAY

COURIERS on horses and camels ride out from the citadel in
all directions spreading the new decree of the king.

INT. MORDECAI'S HOME - MORNING

Mordecai enters his home. His wife -- ADINA -- and his
adopted daughter HADASSAH -- who is ESTHER -- greet him and
are happy that he is home.

Esther is a stunning beautiful seventeen year old girl. Her
beauty and maturity far exceed her age.

Mordecai slumps into the house. He carries no bag, but looks as if he carries the world on his shoulders.

He drops into a chair and sits with his hands wrapped around his head.

> ESTHER
> Father, what troubles you? Is it
> not the day the Lord has made?
> Shall we not be filled with joy,
> rejoicing and being glad for it?

Mordecai takes a long pause before finally responding. <u>It is taking all of his energy to speak of what he has learned.</u>

> MORDECAI
> My child, it is well that you have
> such faith and such joy, for news
> has come that will affect you
> deeply and it will take such as
> that to carry you through.

> ADINA
> Mordecai, what is it that is so
> dire?

> MORDECAI
> I have come from sitting at the
> king's gate and have heard news of
> a new decree.

> ESTHER
> What is it?

> MORDECAI
> It appears the king longs for the
> queen. I have seen him stroll the
> grounds, lost in her memory.

> ESTHER
> Why does he not just let her
> return?

> MORDECAI
> My child. Once the king has
> established a decree, it cannot be
> reversed.

> ESTHER
> So what is the new decree?

MORDECAI
All young virgins must be brought
to the palace and prepared for his
viewing. From them a new queen
shall be chosen.

ADINA
Surely the king would not want a
Hebrew girl. Wouldn't that be
forbidden?

ESTHER
It shall not matter, because I will
not go.

MORDECAI
You have no choice, child. The king
has made his decree. All of his
subjects must obey. Why, look what
happen to Queen Vashti when she
disobeyed.

ADINA
Is there nothing you can do
Mordecai?

MORDECAI
Me? What authority do I hold with
the king? I sit at his gate and
that is all. He does not know that
I live. No, Hadassah, must go.

ESTHER
I may be forced to go, but I do not
have to make myself of notice once
I am there. I am sure there will be
much more beautiful girls then I.
He shall surely choose one of them
and I shall be home to you before
the month's end.

Mordecai looks down at his hands in silence.

MORDECAI
No Hadassah. I am afraid you will
not return to this home.

ADINA
What do you mean Mordecai? Why not?

                    MORDECAI
          Those that are not chosen to be
          queen are still subjects of the
          king and will most likely live out
          their days in his harem as a
          concubine.

Adina hugs Esther and the two begin crying.

                    MORDECAI
          I wish that it were not so
          daughter. Thankfully there is none
          more lovely in this land than you.
          I suspect the king will have one
          look at you and crown you
          instantly.

                    ESTHER
          Spoken like a father, not a king.

Mordecai smiles at Esther.

                    MORDECAI
          To be safe, Hadassah, you must not
          let anyone know that you are
          Hebrew. You shall go by the name
          Esther once you enter the palace.

EXT. SHUSHAN CITADEL - DAY

Caravans are entering the citadel loaded with beautiful young
women from across the land.

The women are unloaded, like cattle, and handed over to
HEGAI. Hegai is a stout, muscular man. Not tall, but powerful
in presence.

As each woman passes into the palace grounds her name is
written down.

Hundreds of women have been brought to the palace and there
is a long line of them as they wait to be allowed to enter.

Many are crying.

Some are holding each other.

Others seem to be happy to be there.

EXT. SHUSHAN CITY STREETS - DAY

Mordecai is walking Esther to the Citadel.

                    MORDECAI
          Hadassah...Esther, promise me that
          you will behave when you enter the
          palace.

                    ESTHER
          I promise father.

                    MORDECAI
          You honor me. I have raised you as
          my own daughter and so you are.

                    ESTHER
          I have only ever known you as my
          father.

                    MORDECAI
          You were so young. We had already
          suffered so much under
          Nebuchadnezzar. I could not bear to
          see you lost after my brother's
          death.

                    ESTHER
          Father, you have taught me our
          history and tradition well. I shall
          never forget it. I know from where
          I come and who my people are.

                    MORDECAI
          Every day I shall pray for you and
          wait to hear word of your well-
          being. Let me bless you now.

The two stop before they get to close to the line of girls
entering the palace.

                    MORDECAI
          Father of Abraham, Isaac, and
          Jacob, go with Hadassah now. I pray
          a father's blessing upon her, that
          she have strength and wisdom and
          that her faith would be made
          strong. Your will be done to your
          child. Amen.

                    ESTHER
          Thank you father.

                    MORDECAI
          Only the Lord knows what lies ahead
          for you, but He will give you the
          strength to see it through.

                         ESTHER
                I know. I trust Him.

Esther and Mordecai hug and she walks away from him.

As she enters the line of young girls she looks back to wave
one last time to her father, <u>knowing there is a chance she
may never see him again.</u>

She wipes a tear away and hides her tears from the other
girls.

Mordecai watches from a distance as Esther is allowed into
the palace walls, and then <u>she is gone.</u>

EXT. OUTER COURT OF THE HOUSE OF THE WOMEN - DAY

The girls that have been allowed to enter the citadel grounds
are being escorted to tables where various perfumes, powders,
oils, and beauty preparations are waiting for them.

The items are selected for them and placed in a basket which
the escorting eunuchs carry for each of the girls.

Esther enters the grounds and is immediately struck by the
beauty of the palace grounds. The gardens of the outer court
are trimmed and immaculate. Flowering trees and shrubs of
numerous varieties surround an ornate tiled walkway and
fountains too numerous to count fill the air with the soft
sound of WATER SPLASHING.

The palace itself is also a stunning work of art and an
architectural feat. Arches of incredibly intricate lattice
work are accented with even more ornate painted tile of rich
colors.

Hegai notices that Esther is admiring the beauty of the
palace. Whereas all of the others are engrossed in the gifts.

<u>Esther stands out from the others because of her wholesome
beauty and humility.</u>

Some of the other girls are screeching and acting jealously
towards one another. Rudely snatching vials of oil from each
other, while others are unable to function due to
uncontrollable crying and wailing.

Hegai leaves his place at the door, placing another in charge
and approaches Esther.

                         HEGAI
                It is lovely.

Esther is startled.

                  ESTHER
      Oh. Yes, very much. I do not
      believe I have seen anything so
      beautiful.

                  HEGAI
      Where do you come from?

                  ESTHER
        (guardedly)
      I am from Shu...Susa.

Esther catches herself from pronouncing the city in the
Hebrew rather than the Persian.

                  HEGAI
      What do you find the most beautiful
      part of this courtyard?

                  ESTHER
      I don't know. It is all so lovely.

Esther looks around her.

                ESTHER (CONT'D)
      I do not think there is one part
      more lovely than another. What
      makes this place so special is the
      culmination of the parts. If you
      begin to look only at a single
      element, then you miss the beauty
      of the whole and I am sure the
      purpose of the design.

Hegai is impressed by her answer and smiles.

He motions for Hathach, who is standing near by watching the
overall proceedings, to come over to them.

                  HEGAI
      Hathach, take...
        (to Esther)
      What is your name?

                  ESTHER
      Esther.

                  HEGAI
      I want you to escort Esther to
      gather her preparations. When you
      do, make sure you gather double for
      her.

                    HATHACH
          It will be done.

                    HEGAI
          And, Hathach, I also want you to
          gather for her a special bundle
          which I have set aside. It is
          filled with the fragrant blossoms
          of every flower from this garden.
          You will find it under the last
          table.

                    ESTHER
          That is most kind, but you do not
          need to do that. I will take just
          what the other girls are given.

                    HEGAI
          Esther. I find you to be a special
          beauty, beyond the others brought
          here today. I believe the king will
          find you to his liking.

Esther blushes. <u>She is humble and modest.</u>

                    ESTHER
          You honor me.

                    HEGAI
          Hathach, I want Esther placed in
          the best house and I want seven
          choice maidservants from the king's
          palace brought here at once to wait
          on her and see to her preparations.
          Do you understand?

                    HATHACH
          Yes Hegai. It shall be done as you
          command.

Esther does not speak for fear of betraying her emotions. But
she bows out of courtesy for the great favor she has received
from Hegai.

                    HEGAI
          Go now. Hathach shall see to all I
          have said and he shall stay near
          you during the preparation.

Hathach leads Esther away as Hegai watches after them before
returning to his place at the gate to greet the young girls
still being brought in.

INT. MORDECAI'S HOME - DUSK

Mordecai is at home eating dinner with Adina.

They are sitting quietly, both lost in thought. The meal is simple.

There is an empty space at the table where Esther used to sit.

> MORDECAI
> I can't stand not knowing. That
> child has not been out of this home
> one night before this.

> ADINA
> Mordecai, for a man of such great
> faith, you certainly worry a lot.

> MORDECAI
> There is much to worry about
> woman...
> (calms down)
> But, you are correct...Worry gains
> us nothing.

> ADINA
> Hadassah is a smart girl. She will
> be fine.

> MORDECAI
> It is so, but I pray she keeps her
> wits about her to keep secret her
> true identity. If they find out she
> is Hebrew...I shudder to think what
> will happen to her.

Adina nods. Concern is etched across her face as well, but she knows better than to voice it.

INT. ESTHER'S QUARTERS SHUSHAN CITADEL - NIGHT

Esther is surrounded by the SEVEN MAIDSERVANTS as they prepare her for sleep.

One is combing her hair, another is perfuming her skin with fine oil.

Another is washing her feet.

In the background two maids are preparing her bedding.

The last two are holding food and drink for her to choose from.

Standing by the door is Hathach.

Esther is in fine spirits and laughing with the maids. The mood is light.

> ESTHER
> Honestly, I have need for nothing else this evening. You girls are spoiling me.

> MAIDSERVANT 1
> My lady, it is why we are here.

> ESTHER
> What? To spoil me rotten so no man could ever please me?

The maids all giggle.

> ESTHER
> Please, just sit with me. This is my first night away from home and more than fine oil, I could simply use friends tonight. If you are truly under my command now, then please, all of you, just sit with me and let us talk.

The maids finish what they are doing and gather to sit around Esther. She sits on the same level with them, not above them.

Hathach watches from his position.

> ESTHER
> Hathach, can you please leave us? I am certain that we will bore you with what we wish to speak about, and it is for a ladies ears anyway.

The maids all giggle again.

Hathach does not smile or react, but bows and leaves the room.

INT. HALL OUTSIDE ESTHER'S QUARTERS

As Hathach closes the door a loud burst of laughter is heard. He grimaces and stands guard in front of the door.

Hegai passes Hathach and notices he is standing in the hall.

                    HEGAI
          Hathach? Why do you stand outside
          Esther's quarters?

                    HATHACH
          The young lady excused me from the
          room.

                    HEGAI
          Why?

                    HATHACH
          Apparently they wish to discuss
          female things.

                    HEGAI
          You are probably better off out
          here than.

                    HATHACH
          Yes. I believe so.

                    HEGAI
          So...how does the young Esther
          fair?

                    HATHACH
          Esther is unusual. Though she knows
          for what purpose she has been
          brought here, she treats the
          maidservants with as much respect
          as they treat her. At times, she
          seems almost embarrassed that they
          are in charge to care for her.

                    HEGAI
          Keep a watchful eye Hathach. Esther
          is a unique girl and I want her
          well prepared for the king.

Hathach nods as Hegai leaves.

EXT. SHUSHAN CITY STREETS - DAY

Mordecai is pacing outside of the court of the women's
quarters where Esther is living.

Hathach is walking near Esther who is walking along the halls
overlooking the beautiful courtyard.

She stops when she notices Mordecai pacing outside the
courtyard. She stares down at him for some time, lost in
thought.

Hathach follows her gaze and also sees Mordecai.

Esther realizes she is staring and catches herself. She looks back at Hathach, and smiles a weak smile.

He does not react and simply looks at her.

She turns away and continues walking along. She hides her face and the tears that are running down her cheek.

Hathach looks back at Mordecai pacing as he follows behind Esther.

INT. WOMAN'S QUARTERS SHUSHAN CITADEL - DAY

All of the virgins are in one very large room. It is as lovely inside this hall as the outer courtyard is.

Hegai is about to address the women.

Eunuchs stand guard around all four walls watching the women who have now gathered themselves into groups. Some groups are together based on the province they came from, others seem to have grouped based on personality type.

Esther is set apart from the others and sits with her entourage of maidservants.

Many of the other girls stare at Esther with jealousy and contempt.

                    HEGAI
          Ladies! Today is the first day of
          your year long preparation before
          you will be allowed to have an
          audience before the king.

The girls WHISPER amongst themselves.

                    HEGAI
          You shall not be permitted to leave
          the citadel. All that you require
          will be provided for you. You will
          do as you are told, you will not
          make special requests. Your
          preparation shall include...

MONTAGE SEQUENCE OF SCENES WHILE HEGAI TALKS:

SHOT OF GIRLS BEING BATHED

                    HEGAI
          Special milk and perfume baths...

SHOT OF GIRLS HAVING THEIR HAIR DONE

> HEGAI
> Your hair will be combed daily to
> ensure softness, silkiness, and
> strength...

SHOT OF GIRLS HAVING THEIR MAKE UP APPLIED

> HEGAI
> You shall be taught the art of make
> up in various methods for all
> occasions...

SHOT OF OILS BEING APPLIED

> HEGAI
> You shall have oils of myrrh
> applied to your skin daily for six
> months.

BACK TO SCENE

> HEGAI
> When it is time for you to have
> audience with the king, you shall
> go to him in the evening. You shall
> not return to this home after that
> night, but instead be moved to the
> second home of women and placed
> under the oversight of SHAASHGAZ,
> the king's eunuch who keeps the
> concubines. If the king is
> delighted with you, he will call
> for you by name and only then will
> you be allowed to return to him. If
> anyone approaches the king without
> first being called for, the penalty
> is death.

Hegai leaves the room and the eunuchs begin to usher the
ladies to various rooms.

Hathach gathers Esther and her maids and ushers them from the
hall.

Many of the other girls watch after Esther, <u>wondering why she
is receiving special treatment.</u>

INT. ESTHER'S ROOM - DAY

Esther is being groomed by her seven maidservants. One is
rubbing her skin with oil, while another combs her hair. They
are all laughing and having a good time.

Hathach stands near the door watching. He seems unamused and
distant -- his normal appearance.

There is a knock on the door and Hathach answers it, letting
the other maidservants enter with trays of food.

                    ESTHER
          Oh my goodness! All that food
          cannot be just for me.

                    MAIDSERVANT 1
          Yes. We must make sure you are well
          fed, to be presentable to the king.

                    ESTHER
          So you plan to present me to him as
          a bloated hog?

The maids laugh.

                    ESTHER
          Come, all of you must join me. I
          cannot possibly eat all of this,
          and nothing should go to waste or
          spoil.

The maids take a break from grooming Esther and they all
gather round the serving trays which are piled with food.

Esther lets the others eat first even though she is the
position of authority.

As the other girls begin to gather food on their plates,
Esther walks over to the window that looks out over the
courtyard.

ESTHER'S POV

She looks down to see Mordecai pacing outside the walls.

BACK TO SCENE

Hathach comes up behind Esther to see what she is looking at.
When he speaks he startles Esther.

                HATHACH
Who is that man? I have seen him
every day since you have arrived
here.

                ESTHER
     (pausing)
That is Mordecai. He is a...friend.
He sits at the king's gate, but
apparently his time is spent
worrying over me now.

Esther walks away leaving Hathach to watch Mordecai pacing.

                MAIDSERVANT 1
Come Esther, we have prepared a
plate for you. Eat with us.

Esther joins the others and looks at her plate. It is filled
with an assortment of delicious items, from meats, and
onions, to dates and fruits.

She picks at the food on her plate and recognizes that some
of the items are not foods that a Jewish girl should eat. <u>She
must eat them so as not to give away who she is.</u>

She smiles and begins to eat with the girls.

EXT. SHUSHAN CITY STREETS

Mordecai is outside the walls of the women's courtyard
pacing.

The door to the courtyard opens and Hathach steps out.

Mordecai sees him and approaches when Hathach beckons for him
to come near.

                HATHACH
You are a friend of Esther's?

Mordecai is surprised that he is known by Hathach. He is
cautious of Hathach.

                MORDECAI
Yes. How is she? Is she well?

                HATHACH
She is very well indeed. She has
received the favor of Hegai the
custodian of the women.

                    MORDECAI
          That is good?

                    HATHACH
          Yes. She sleeps in the finest room,
          eats the finest foods, and has
          seven maidservants looking after
          her every need.

                    MORDECAI
          Thank you for this news.

                    HATHACH
          As I have news and I see you, I
          will tell you.

                    MORDECAI
          Thank you.

Mordecai leaves and Hathach goes back into the citadel.

INT. THE THRONE ROOM

King Ahasuerus sits on his thrown facing his princes
including the vizier Haman, Tarshish, Memucan, and Admatha.

The room is charged as the men are in a serious debate.

Standing by the doors are two eunuchs - BIGTHAN and TERESH.
Both men have strong powerful arms, but do not look to be the
brightest men.

                    HAMAN
          My king, I beseech you this day to
          heed my warning.

                    TARSHISH
          There is no reason to believe what
          you are telling us Haman. To me it
          sounds like old bad blood.

The other princes nod in agreement.

The king is sitting listening.

                    HAMAN
          My princess, and king, while it is
          true that the Amalekites, my
          people, have been wronged by the
          Jews, it is not for this that I
          bring you this concern.

                    TARSHISH
          But you have not provided any good
          reason for us to fear the Jews now.
          They live among us freely and many
          are prospering. For what offense do
          you see them committing?

                    HAMAN
          I fear that they will multiply and
          soon overcome the king. If there
          are too many of them, they will not
          honor our king. They already do not
          serve our gods. Their laws are not
          our laws.

There is some agreement between the princes on this account.

                    KING AHASUERUS
          Enough. I have heard enough today.
          Haman, I have heard your complaint
          and it is noted.

                    HAMAN
          Yes my king.

                    KING AHASUERUS
          Is there any other business we must
          attend to?

                    ADMATHA
          My King there is the matter of the
          guards of the citadel.

                    KING AHASUERUS
          What do they seek now?

                    MEMUCAN
          They have asked that their food
          allowance be increased.

                    KING AHASUERUS
          Again! It would seem all these men
          do is eat. When do they have time
          to guard?

The princes look back at the door where Bigthan and Teresh
stand.

Neither guard reacts or moves.

                    KING AHASUERUS
          I have heard enough for today.

INT. HAREM HALL

Hegai is overseeing the women's preparations.

The room is filled with all of the girls to be presented to
the king, each are in various states of preparation.

Some are trying on, or looking, at clothes.

Some are being taught how to apply make-up.

Still others are smelling various fragrances.

Esther approaches Hegai.

                    ESTHER
          Hegai, if I may.

                    HEGAI
          Of course.

                    ESTHER
          We have spent weeks now learning to
          apply our make-up and comb our
          hair, honestly how many ways are
          their to do either?

                    HEGAI
          What is it that you would want to
          learn?

                    ESTHER
          It would seem that more important
          than just our beauty would be to
          learn what is truly important to
          the king?

                    HEGAI
          For someone so young, you have
          great wisdom. You are the first to
          ever ask me such a question.

                    ESTHER
          And yet, it is the most important,
          is it not?

                    HEGAI
          So it is.

                    ESTHER
          Then please, I ask that you tell me
          the secrets of the king so I may be
          more pleasing to him.

Hegai smiles and begins to lead Esther away from the others.

> HEGAI
> Walk with me and I shall give you
> the wisdom you seek.

The two leave the hall.

EXT. COURTYARD - DAY

Hegai and Esther are walking through the courtyard. Hathach
is not far behind them. We cannot hear them talking, but
Hegai is speaking at length to Esther MOS.

EXT. KING'S GATE - DAY

Mordecai is sitting within the gate of the citadel.

People are passing through the open gate and conducting
business.

There are other Jewish men sitting with him.

The place where they sit is a great stone hewn square where
people come to have their problems listened to and resolved.
Mordecai is one that helps resolve the people's issues.

> SANHEDRIN 1
> Mordecai, how is Hadassah?

> MORDECAI
> I received reports that she is
> doing very well. She has even
> changed her attitude and is now
> looking forward to meeting the
> king.

> SANHEDRIN 2
> That is good?

> MORDECAI
> I hope so. The king is easily
> swayed and there is rumor that
> Haman is calling for our heads.

The other Sanhedrin nod in agreement then shake their heads
to show their displeasure with the news.

> MORDECAI
> We must continue to pray for her
> safety and God's will in this
> situation.

The other's all nod in agreement.

INT. HAREM HALL - DAY

TEXT FADES IN OVER THE SCENE - "TEN MONTHS LATER"

The women have been gathered in the harem hall again. They
are all more lovely than when they first arrived and much
more disciplined.

Hegai is addressing the women.

Behind him are large purple cloaks that cover piles of
something on tables. The tables stretch the length of the
room and eunuchs stand behind the tables.

> HEGAI
> Your preparations are nearly
> complete.

The women GIGGLE and WHISPER between themselves.

Esther sits quietly in the corner with her maidservants and
Hathach.

> HEGAI
> Today, you shall each be allowed to
> pick one item from the king's
> treasure for your own that you may
> wear when you are presented to the
> king.

The eunuchs remove the purple cloaks that were covering the
huge piles of gold and jeweled items. The tables are piled
high with tiaras, necklaces, bracelets, rings, and other
riches.

The women are besides themselves with glee as they look upon
the riches that they will be allowed to choose from.

> HEGAI
> I recommend that you chose wisely.
> Soon we shall begin to present you
> to the king.

All of the women rush the tables and begin to pick through
the items. The room is filled with the SQUEALS and SCREAMS of
the ladies who behave as if they have never seen such riches,
which of course most have not.

Esther has not moved from her seat. She watches as the other
women swarm the table like locust on a field.

Hegai approaches her.

                    HEGAI
          Esther, will you not be choosing
          something for yourself?

                    ESTHER
          I would no idea what to choose.

                    HEGAI
          So what will you do?

                    ESTHER
          If I have learned anything in these
          many months, Hegai, it is to seek
          the wisdom and counsel of those
          that know more than me.

Esther smiles at Hegai who returns the gesture.

                    HEGAI
          Wait here.

Hegai walks over to the tables of riches and picks through
the items.

Esther watches and waits.

Eventually Hegai returns with a beautiful yet humble necklace
made of gold and encrusted with many tiny jewels.

                    HEGAI
          I happen to know this is one of the
          king's favorite pieces. It will
          surely catch his eye as much as you
          do.

Hegai places the necklace on Esther.

                    ESTHER
          Hegai, you have blessed me yet
          again.

INT. ESTHER'S ROOM - NIGHT

Esther is looking out at the courtyard. She is fingering the
necklace which she is still wearing.

Her maidservants are in the room preparing her bed.

We see some of the girls being lead to the royal palace to
meet the king.

Others are being lead to the second home of the women -- that of the royal concubines. Some of these girls being led to the second home are in tears.

One of the maids approaches Esther.

> MAIDSERVANT 1
> Don't worry Esther. I am sure you will find grace and favor with the king.

> ESTHER
> Thank you. It is the waiting the bothers me most.

> MAIDSERVANT 1
> Yes.

> ESTHER
> It seems like we have already waited a lifetime and now we must wait longer for our turn to come.

> MAIDSERVANT 1
> I am sure it will be your time soon.

The maid leaves Esther to her thoughts.

INT. THE THRONE ROOM

Hegai is standing before the king.

On the edges of the throne room are THE SCRIBES and the princes of the provinces.

> KING AHASUERUS
> Hegai, I do not care to recount the number of girls I have meet these past few nights but none have captured my eye.

> HEGAI
> I understand my king.

> KING AHASUERUS
> Is there not one that I can hope to call queen?

> HEGAI
> I believe there is.

                    KING AHASUERUS
          Then what do you wait for? Why have
          I not met this girl yet?

                    HEGAI
          Tonight my king. I shall make sure
          she is presented to you tonight.

Hegai backs out of the thrown room.

After Hegai leaves, Ahasuerus turns to his guards.

                    KING AHASUERUS
          Call in Haman.

One of the guards exits the room and returns moments later
with Haman.

Haman approaches the king.

                    KING AHASUERUS
          Ah Haman. How is my friend today?

                    HAMAN
          I am well my king.

                    KING AHASUERUS
          There is much I wish to discuss
          with you. Come, sit with me.

                    HAMAN
          Yes my king. As you wish.

                    KING AHASUERUS
          I know there has been much that has
          been troubling your heart lately. I
          wish for you to tell me more.

                    HAMAN
          Thank you.

EXT. OUTSIDE THE WOMAN'S COURTYARD - LATE AFTERNOON

Hathach is visiting with Mordecai again at the doorway.

                    HATHACH
          Tonight Esther shall be presented
          to the king.

                    MORDECAI
          Is she well?

                    HATHACH
          She finds favor with everyone she
          meets. There is not one in the
          palace that does not think she
          should be the queen.

                    MORDECAI
          That is my Esther.

                    HATHACH
          I must return to her. I shall meet
          you again tomorrow to let you know
          how tonight goes.

                    MORDECAI
          Yes, thank you.

The two shake hands. There is a bond forming between the two
men.

Mordecai leaves and Hathach goes back inside the court.

INT. ESTHER'S ROOM - NIGHT

Hegai enter's Esther's room.

The maidservants all bow to him and move away revealing
Esther who is stunningly beautiful in a lovely gown. Her hair
has been freshly combed. Her make-up is flawless. She is
amazingly beautiful. She is wearing the necklace that Hegai
picked out for her.

As Hegai sees her he tries not to react.

He turns to Hathach who cannot hide his smile.

Hegai turns back to Esther.

                    ESTHER
          Is it time?

                    HEGAI
          Yes.

                    ESTHER
          Thank you Hegai. I have my friends
          to thank...and you for all of your
          kindness and counsel.

                    HEGAI
          Are you ready?

                    ESTHER
          As ready as I will ever be.

                    HEGAI
          Then let us go.

Hegai turns to leave and Esther follows. As he approaches the
door Hegai looks at Hathach and smiles.

INT. HALLS OF THE PALACE - NIGHT

Hegai is leading Esther to the king's chambers.

Everyone they pass smiles at Esther and bows. She always
returns their smiles.

                    HEGAI
          Do not be nervous.

Esther doesn't speak.

                    HEGAI
          I can tell you, that the king has
          not been pleased with any of the
          previous girls.

                    ESTHER
          Is our king that difficult to
          please?

                    HEGAI
          Until now I suspect.

Hegai smiles at Esther who smiles weakly.

They finally reach the King's chambers.

Hegai knocks.

                    KING AHASUERUS (O.S.)
               (heard from inside)
          Enter.

Hegai opens the door and peaks his head in.

                    HEGAI
          My king it is Hegai, I have for you
          Esther of Susa.

We hear the king but still have not entered the room or seen
him.

> KING AHASUERUS (O.S.)
> Send her in.

Hegai opens the door and moves aside so Esther can enter.

INT. THE KING'S CHAMBERS - NIGHT

Esther enters the chambers.

Candles are lit through-out the room, casting an orange-yellow light. A slight breeze moves the few sheer curtains. Moonlight floods the room and adds a blue tint to the areas not light by the candles.

A larger bed fills one part of the room. Other furniture includes a desk and chairs including a few chaise lounges.

Esther slowly enters the room, stopping in the middle. She looks around to find the king.

Ahasuerus is watching Esther as she enters the room.

> ESTHER
> My king?

> KING AHASUERUS
> Do not be frightened. Come closer.

> ESTHER
> I'm not frightened, but I do not
> see you.

> KING AHASUERUS
> You're not afraid?

> ESTHER
> Do I have reason to be? I know you
> to be a kind king. Fair and honest.
> Certainly if I should dishonor you,
> I would have reason to be fearful,
> but...

> KING AHASUERUS
> But?

> ESTHER
> I do not plan to do such a thing.

Ahasuerus enters the light so he can be seen for the first time.

Esther is startled as this is the first time she has seen the him.

He is dressed in fine clothes and is handsome and strong. His hair is combed and oiled.

                    KING AHASUERUS
          Do I startle you?

Esther blushes and looks away.

                    ESTHER
          My king is more handsome than I had
          thought.

                    KING AHASUERUS
          Flattery...that will get you
          everywhere with the king.

He smiles and approaches Esther. He is looking her up and down.

                    ESTHER
          I don't mean to flatter.

                    KING AHASUERUS
          You don't? Do you wish to insult?

                    ESTHER
          You twist my words. I just meant to
          say, that the king is pleasant to
          the eyes which any queen would hope
          for.

                    KING AHASUERUS
          So am I now on presentation?

                    ESTHER
          Not at all my king, but wouldn't
          you wish your queen to be happy
          with you as well. It makes it that
          much more appealing for the queen
          to please the king.

                    KING AHASUERUS
          Ha. Indeed. And would you please
          this king?

Esther is bold now while still being respectful.

                    ESTHER
          I would do as the king wishes and
          always honor him.

Ahasuerus nods his approval and continues to circle Esther, like a hunter circles his prey.

                    KING AHASUERUS
          Hegai spoke true, you are lovely.

                    ESTHER
          Thank you my king. I dare say a
          year of preparation could make even
          a pig look attractive.

                    KING AHASUERUS
                    (laughing)
          I am not so sure. I have seen many
          girls before you and I am not sure
          a year was long enough.

The two share a laugh. The two relax.

Ahasuerus sits on one of the chaise lounges and motions for
Esther to do the same.

                    KING AHASUERUS
          Come, Esther, sit with me.

Esther moves with grace to a seat across from the king.

He watches her every move.

Before she sits, Esther notices a vessel of wine and two
glasses.

                    ESTHER
          Would my king like some wine?

                    KING AHASUERUS
          Yes, that would be good, but just a
          taste. I wish to be sober this
          night so I can remember every
          detail.

                    ESTHER
          Now my king flatters me.

                    KING AHASUERUS
          Does it work on maidens, as well as
          kings?

Esther simply smiles over her shoulder to him as she pours
him a cup of wine.

She brings him the drink and then sits across form him.

He sips the wine and watches her.

                    KING AHASUERUS
          Have you enjoyed your time in the
          palace?

                    ESTHER
          Aside from being separated from my
          family, the time here is simple
          enough. We sit around being
          pampered all day and taught how to
          be beautiful.

                    KING AHASUERUS
          Do you always speak your mind so
          freely?

                    ESTHER
          I'm sorry my king. I am out of
          order.

                    KING AHASUERUS
          No I assure you, it is somewhat
          refreshing to hear such truth
          spoken. The others go on and on
          about how happy they are, but I can
          tell they are dishonest with their
          answers.

                    ESTHER
          My king, I am pleased to be here.

EXT. KING'S GATE - DAY

Mordecai is sitting with the Sanhedrin at the king's gate. It
is another day in the life.

A young scribe from the royal court runs up to Mordecai and
hands him a slip of paper, then turns and runs back to the
palace.

Mordecai unrolls the note and reads it.

The others look on.

                    SANHEDRIN 2
          Mordecai, is everything all right?

Mordecai is silent as he takes his time rereading the
message, trying to truly grasp its meaning.

                    SANHEDRIN 2
          Mordecai?

Mordecai stands and begins to leave.

                    SANHEDRIN 2 (CONT'D)
          Mordecai!?

Mordecai turns back to the group.

                    MORDECAI
          I'm sorry my friends. It would
          appear the king is going to make a
          very important announcement today.
          I must get home at once.

                    SANHEDRIN 2
          But...

Mordecai is off at a quick pace for such an old man.

The other Sanhedrin are left to shrug and look at each other
wondering.

INT. THE THRONE ROOM - DAY

The king is sitting on his throne and the room is filled with
scribes, the seven princes, Haman, and many more people of
the royal court. Mordecai and the Sanhedrin are also in
attendance.

Ahasuerus is smiling and seems very happy. He has not looked
this happy since the opening feast.

The room is A BUZZ WITH CHATTER of what the announcement will
be.

The king motions for the attendant to quiet the room.

                    ATTENDANT
          Attention.

The room quickly becomes silent. All eyes turn to the king.

                    ATTENDANT
          On this day in the month of Tebeth,
          in the seventh year of the reign of
          King Ahasuerus, the king wishes to
          announce the selection and crowning
          of his new queen.

The room fills with CHATTER again. The crowd is excited to
see the new queen.

                    ATTENDANT
          Presenting to the court, Queen
          Esther.

The doors at the far end of the room, across from the throne, open and Esther stands there, as lovely as ever, in a full length gown. The gown has an appearance of being both royal and also a wedding gown.

She is stunning in appearance as she glides down the middle of the room towards the throne.

Ahasuerus stands as Esther gets closer.

Mordecai is torn between his happiness and concern. He hides his emotions as best he can.

Once Esther reaches the steps to the throne, the king reaches down to help her up the steps.

When she reaches the top level, she kneels before the king.

The attendant hands the King a crown covered in jewels which he places on Esther's head.

She rises and turns to the crowd, who cheer and applaud.

The attendant steps forward as Ahasuerus and Esther take their places on the thrones.

> ATTENDANT
> In accordance with the king's
> wishes, it is decreed that today be
> a holiday in all the provinces.
> Gifts according to the generosity
> of the king shall be given to the
> officials and servants, and tonight
> shall be a great feast, to here by
> be known as the Feast of Esther.

The crowd erupts in applause and cheers.

Ahasuerus takes Esther's hand and smiles at her, then the crowd.

INT. ROYAL HALL - NIGHT

The Feast of Esther is in full regal. There is much food and music being enjoyed by the large crowd. All of the princes and Haman are in attendance along with hundreds of others.

Hathach stands nearby along with Hegai.

Ahasuerus is sitting with Esther.

> KING AHASUERUS
> Are you enjoying your feast?

                    ESTHER
          Would it offend the king if I said
          I was a bit embarrassed that all
          this in named after me?

                    KING AHASUERUS
          A humble queen? I am not sure I
          have ever been in the presence of
          one such as yourself.

                    ESTHER
          Is that a good thing?

                    KING AHASUERUS
          Very.

Esther reaches out and takes the king's hand in hers.

                    ESTHER
          You have honored me today and
          tonight, with this feast.

Esther surveys the hall.

                    ESTHER
          I am proud to be named your queen,
          and will do all in my power to live
          up to such an honor.

                    KING AHASUERUS
          Esther, it is I that should be
          thanking you.

                    ESTHER
          My king?

                    KING AHASUERUS
          Ask my attendants. I have been
          filled with such gloom and sadness.
          You have brought joy back to what
          had become a darkened heart.

A new SONG with a rapid tempo begins to play and the room
begins to swirl with motion as the guests start dancing a
traditional dance, holding one another's hands and moving
around the room in a circle, while facing in.

                    KING AHASUERUS
          Shall we join them?

                    ESTHER
          I...I am not familiar with this
          dance.

                    KING AHASUERUS
          Come Esther, look at it. How hard
          can it be for you to learn. Dance
          with me! Tonight we rejoice.

Ahasuerus takes Esther by the hands and leads her down to the
dancing.

They enter the ring and begin moving along with the circle.

The music's tempo speeds up and the circle moves faster and
faster.

INT. THE KING'S CHAMBERS - NIGHT

It is dark but for a few candles. Moonlight is the main
source of illumination.

Ahasuerus enters the chambers wearing pants. His chest is
bear.

Esther also enters the chamber wearing a long silken gown.
The moonlight highlights her lovely form.

The two meet in the center of the room and embrace in a
passionate kiss.

He sweeps her up into his arms and carries her to the bed.

As their passion burns hotter, the flame of one of the
candles also seems to burn brighter and hotter than before,
blocking the view of the bed.

EXT. KING'S GATE - DAY

Mordecai is sitting in his normal place within the king's
gate speaking with the Sanhedrin. There is the normal bustle
of traffic coming and going.

                    MORDECAI
          It was a lovely night and feast. I
          am so proud.

                    SANHEDRIN 1
          As well you should be Mordecai. It
          was a glorious occasion.

The Sanhedrin are distracted by another conversation and
turns to listen.

Mordecai sits basking in the joy of what has transpired.

Two of the king's guards, Bigthan and Teresh, are passing by Mordecai, deep in serious conversation. They are unaware of Mordecai and their speech is loud enough that he can hear them.

> BIGTHAN
> So the plan is ready?

> TERESH
> Yes. Soon the king will see that we deserve our fair share of the food.

As they walk past Mordecai, he follows them because of what he has heard. He stays close enough to listen, but not so that he is discovered.

> BIGTHAN
> You have the disguises ready for us?

> TERESH
> Yes. We shall slip in and lay hands on the king while he sleeps. When no guards come to his aid he will realize the foolishness of his decision.

> BIGTHAN
> Good. And the others are with us?

> TERESH
> Yes. We are all in agreement.

> BIGTHAN
> Then before this day is done it shall be completed.

Mordecai drifts away from them and heads back toward the citadel.

EXT. OUTER COURT OF THE HOUSE OF THE WOMEN - DAY

Queen Esther is walking the courtyard enjoying the beauty of the gardens. She looks happy.

Hathach is with her, a few steps behind.

There is a commotion at the gate and the two turn to see what it is.

Mordecai is there.

>   MORDECAI
>   I must speak with the queen, it is
>   urgent!

>   GUARD
>   No one passes that is not first
>   invited.

>   MORDECAI
>   But this is a matter of grave
>   importance.

Esther rushes over to the gate.

Hathach excuses the guard and allows Esther the privacy she needs.

>   ESTHER
>   Father, what is it?

>   MORDECAI
>   I have over heard two of the king's
>   guards as they discuss their plans
>   to lay hands on the king.

>   ESTHER
>   What?!

Esther's reaction cause Hathach to step closer so he can hear the conversation.

>   ESTHER
>   When? How?

>   MORDECAI
>   Tonight. They plan to attack him
>   while he sleeps. I fear for your
>   safety as well.

>   ESTHER
>   Do not fear. I shall let the king
>   know at once.

Esther turns to leave and Hathach nods his approval to Mordecai.

Mordecai watches as Esther rushes into the palace.

INT. THE KING'S CHAMBERS - NIGHT

Ahasuerus and Esther are asleep. The room is dark.

Two shadows slip into the room and approach the bed. As they draw near, suddenly the room is filled with motion as Hathach and other guards surround the two assailants and take hold of them.

King Ahasuerus rises from the bed and approaches the two wound be attackers.

He unmasks them and slaps Bigthan.

Without another word and only a sweep of his hand Bigthan and Teresh are roughly carried away.

Esther, who is kneeling on the bed, hugs Ahasuerus and they kiss.

> KING AHASUERUS
> Thank you my queen. It was exactly
> as you warned me.

> ESTHER
> I am just pleased that you are
> safe. I do not wish to be a widow
> my first month of marriage.

> KING AHASUERUS
> Nor do I wish to make you one.

Esther shivers from the adrenaline.

Ahasuerus notices and place his arm and a sheet around her.

> KING AHASUERUS
> Are you cold?

> ESTHER
> I am not used to this type of
> intrigue. I admit I was afraid for
> my king.

> KING AHASUERUS
> There was no need for fear. Aside
> from the dozens of guards that
> surrounded us, I assure you I have
> not let myself grow soft. I would
> not allow anything to happen to me.

Esther looks at him quizzically.

> KING AHASUERUS
> (jokingly)
> Or you of course.

                    ESTHER
          You joke.

                    KING AHASUERUS
          Of course. You are so serious. I
          wanted to see you smile again. It
          brings me peace.

                    ESTHER
          Being your queen makes me smile.

                    KING AHASUERUS
          Then this is a perfect arrangement.
          None could be better. It is as if
          the gods have destined it.

Esther smiles.

                    KING AHASUERUS
          So, tell me again, how did you
          learn of this plot?

                    ESTHER
          A man named Mordecai, who sits at
          your gate, overheard the men
          speaking their plans this day.

                    KING AHASUERUS
          And how is it that this Mordecai
          came to you with the plot?

Esther hesitates as she must think of a reasonable answer.

                    ESTHER
          He is friends with Hathach, my
          eunuch. They spoke and Hathach made
          me aware of the plot.

                    KING AHASUERUS
          It is interesting.

                    ESTHER
          What is my king?

                    KING AHASUERUS
          One never knows who will provide
          the information you most need to
          prevail in life. Every person you
          allow to be around you, can either
          bring blessing or tragedy.

Esther reaches up and hugs Ahasuerus.

                    ESTHER
          I hope to only ever bring you great
          blessing.

                    KING AHASUERUS
          And so you do.

The two kiss.

INT. THE THRONE ROOM - DAY

The throne room is filled with scribes and officials, the
princes, Haman, and Mordecai.

                    ATTENDANT
          Let it be entered into the
          chronicles that the king's life was
          saved this day by the queen.

Esther whispers into the king's ear and he nods his
understanding.

He stands.

The attendant continues unaware that the king has stood.

                    ATTENDANT
          The attackers are to hanged by the
          gallows this day...

                    KING AHASUERUS
          For the record, let it be noted
          that Mordecai, brought this matter
          to Queen Esther's attention. It is
          the queen's wish that he should
          receive the honor here today.

King Ahasuerus motions for Mordecai to stand.

The officials and princes cheer enthusiasticals for him.

Ahasuerus raises his hand to quiet the room.

                    KING AHASUERUS
          There is another honor I wish to
          bestow this day.

Ahasuerus motions for Haman to stand.

                    KING AHASUERUS
          Haman, the son of Hammedatha the
          Agagite, for your loyal service to
          this throne I decree it this day
          that your seat shall be above the
          other princes of the province. Your
          word shall be just lower than my
          own.

The officials and princes applaud for Haman, not quite as
enthusiastically as they did for Mordecai.

                    KING AHASUERUS
          Let it be known that Haman should
          be honored by all in my kingdom and
          treated with the same respect that
          you would show me...or my queen.

Ahasuerus proudly looks back at Esther.

The people in the room applaud again with the exception of
Mordecai.

INT. HAMAM'S HOME - NIGHT

Haman is at home with his wife ZERESH. His home is dark but
nice and richly decorated.

Zeresh is darkly attractive with heavy eyeliner above and
beneath her eyes. Her's is an exotic beauty.

Haman is sitting in a high backed chair, almost like a throne
and Zeresh is serving him.

                    ZERESH
          You should be pleased Haman. The
          king has bestowed a great honor on
          you today. Maybe I can do something
          to honor you as well.

Zeresh sits down seductively in Haman's lap.

                    HAMAN
          It is good.

                    ZERESH
          Yet, something still troubles you
          tonight.

                    HAMAN
          Yes, but I am not sure what or why.
          My spirit is anxious.

                    ZERESH
                 (seductively)
            Maybe I can sooth this wicked
            spirit.

                    HAMAN
            There is not doubt you can, but...

                    ZERESH
            If you are so bothered, consult
            your charts. What do they tell you?

Zeresh points to a stack of charts and scrolls that line the
walls. This is the first that we learn that Haman is an
astrologer.

                    HAMAN
            I shall do that.

Haman turns his attention to his wife.

                    HAMAN
            Woman, you are full of wisdom
            aren't you?

                    ZERESH
            That is why you married me.

                    HAMAN
            That is not the only reason.

Haman kisses his wife and they passionately embrace.

INT. MORDECAI'S HOME - NIGHT

A different scene is playing out at Mordecai's home. Mordecai
is pacing like a caged tiger.

                    MORDECAI
            I cannot believe that the king has
            raise up Haman, of all people.

                    ADINA
            Mordecai, come, sit.

                    MORDECAI
            I cannot. I am filled with dread.

                    ADINA
            For someone who was also honored
            today you would think you had been
            sent to the gallows like those
            other men.

Mordecai stops pacing and finally sits down at the table.

                    ADINA
          Come now. How bad can it be
          Mordecai?

Mordecai stands again and resumes his pacing.

                    MORDECAI
          Woman, this Haman has a hatred for
          the Jews that goes back
          generations. Since the time of
          Saul.

                    ADINA
          And what will your pacing do to
          resolve that tonight?

Mordecai stops and looks lovingly at his wife.

                    MORDECAI
          Maybe you should sit at the king's
          gate and dispense wisdom, you are
          better than I it seems.

                    ADINA
          Sit. Eat something. A full stomach
          will ease your anxiousness and
          tomorrow will be a new day.

Mordecai sits down again. Adina serves him dinner.

                    MORDECAI
          My dear wife, you are good for me.

EXT. KING'S GATE - DAY

Mordecai and the Sanhedrin are sitting in their normal place.
The streets are bustling with activity.

STORE OWNERS are peddling their wares, and SHOPPERS are
moving about between the stalls.

HORNS can be heard coming from the citadel.

The crowd parts as soon it becomes apparent that a PARADE is
coming towards the King's gate.

All of the people bow before the approaching procession.

It is Haman, being carried through the city streets because
of his promotion from the King.

Haman sits smugly in a COVERED SEDAN carried on the shoulders of FOUR EUNUCHS. He looks down at all those who he passes with contempt and disdain. On his black tunic is a large embroidered icon of a pagan god in gold and red thread. It can be easily seen.

As he nears the King's gate Haman spots Mordecai. He is the only one still standing.

Haman rises in his seat on the sedan and locks eyes with Mordecai as his procession passes.

Mordecai stands firm in his defiances to bow to Haman.

Haman stops the procession in front of Mordecai. Acting as if no offense has been made, and trying to remain composed Haman addresses Mordecai.

>   HAMAN
>   Peace be upon thee.

>   MORDECAI
>   There is no peace, says the Lord,
>   unto the wicked.

Haman cannot hide his anger and contempt for Mordecai now. The insult has gone to far. He YELLS for the procession to move forward.

The procession passes and the people stand again.

>   SANHEDRIN 1
>   Mordecai, why do you transgress the
>   king's command?

>   MORDECAI
>   Is it not written that man should
>   not kneel to any god but our God?

>   SANHEDRIN 1
>   Yes, but Haman, does not portend to
>   be god.

>   MORDECAI
>   My brothers, did you not see the
>   image on his tunic? It was the
>   image of a false idol. I will never
>   bow to such an image.

INT. HAMAM'S HOME - DAY

Haman is tossing things about his home.

Zeresh watches from a distance but does not try to consul
Haman during his tantrum.

After he has broken a few items and his anger is spent he
sits.

Finally Zeresh moves to comfort her husband.

>   ZERESH
>   My dear Haman. This is such a
>   trivial matter.

>   HAMAN
>   It is not woman! Do you not see how
>   he insulted me?

>   ZERESH
>   Of course my husband, but he is one
>   man. Take care of him.

Haman stares at his wife and what she is implying.

>   HAMAN
>   It is beneath me to lay hands on
>   this simple man.

>   ZERESH
>   Yes, and Mordecai saved the king's
>   life. You cannot ask the king for
>   his direct punishment.

>   HAMAN
>   What then shall I do?

>   ZERESH
>   Did you know he is a Jew?

>   HAMAN
>   Where did you learn this?

>   ZERESH
>   I have asked around. He sits with
>   the Sanhedrin at the King's gate.
>   He socializes with them.

>   HAMAN
>   This is an interesting turn.

>   ZERESH
>   Now you have new reason to bring
>   this before the king. He defied the
>   king's command. Could this be the
>   beginning of an uprising? A revolt?

> HAMAN
> Yes. I can deal with the lot of
> them and him all at once. All the
> Jews - young and old, women and
> little children. He has unknowingly
> set his own trap.

Haman hugs Zeresh.

> HAMAN
> I must cast the stones to determine
> when to destroy them.

Zeresh, as if knowing what Haman would do next, hands him the
stones and clears a place at the table.

Haman cast the first stones and consults his astrological
maps.

He shakes his head in frustration at his findings.

He casts again and again is frustrated.

> HAMAN
> Every day shows some favor for
> these Jews. I must find the perfect
> time.

Haman, consults his charts and the stones again and continues
to be frustrated.

> HAMAN
> Nisan is favorable for the Jews due
> to Passover sacrifice. Iyyar,
> because of the small Passover. Is
> there not a date that favors me?

> ZERESH
> What about Adar?

Haman studies his charts.

> HAMAN
> Yes! It is the sign of Pisces. Now
> I shall be able to swallow them as
> fish which swallow one another.

INT. ESTHER'S ROOM - DAY

Esther is sitting reading. She is surrounded by a few maid
servants who are busy whispering amongst themselves. There
does not seem to be a care in the world for Esther.

Hathach enters the room. He appears anxious and he approaches
Esther.

> HATHACH
> My queen, there is news that is of
> most importance to you.

> ESTHER
> What is it Hathach?

> HATHACH
> Earlier today, during the
> procession for Haman, the man
> Mordecai failed to bow to him. This
> very minute Haman is before the
> king asking for permission to deal
> with the offense.

> ESTHER
> Do you know of what he is asking
> for?

> HATHACH
> No my queen, but I fear it will not
> be good.

> ESTHER
> Go now and learn what else you can.
> Bring word back to me as soon as
> you can.

> HATHACH
> Yes, my queen.

Hathach leaves the room.

Esther looks distressed but tries her best to hide her
emotions. She smiles to the maids and returns to her book,
but she cannot concentrate on the words of the page and
simply stares, deep in thought.

INT. THE THRONE ROOM - DAY

Haman is before the king presenting his case.

The throne room is filled with scribes and the princes and
those of the king's court.

> HAMAN
> There is a certain people scattered
> and dispersed among the people in
> all the provinces of your kingdom;
> (MORE)

                    HAMAN (CONT'D)
          their laws are different from all
          other people's, and they do not
          keep the king's laws. Therefore it
          is not fitting for the king to let
          them remain.

                    KING AHASUERUS
          Who are these people?

                    HAMAN
          The Jews. If it pleases the king,
          let a decree be written that they
          be destroyed, and I will pay ten
          thousand talents of silver into the
          hands of those who do the work.

Ahasuerus considers Haman's request. After a moment he takes
off his signet ring from his hand and gives it to Haman.

                    KING AHASUERUS
          The money and the people are given
          to you, to do with them as seems
          good to you.

                    HAMAN
          Scribes!

                                        CUT TO:

A MONTAGE OF IMAGES of couriers riding out to all of the
provinces delivering the decree of the king to exterminate
the Jews. We see images of the couriers RIDING, STOPPING TO
DELIVER THE MESSAGE, READING THE MESSAGE, PRINCES OF TRIBES
READING THE MESSAGE, JEWS HIDING IN THEIR HOMES, JEWS
GATHERING THEIR BELONGINGS TO FLEE. JEWS TEARING THEIR
CLOTHES AND PUTTING ASHES ON THEIR HEADS. JEWISH WOMEN
WEEPING, AND MANY LAYING IN SACKCLOTH AND ASHES.

                    SCRIBE (V.O.)
          The great King Ahasuerus writes
          thus to the rulers and inferior
          governors of a hundred and twenty-
          seven provinces, from India even to
          Ethiopia, who hold authority under
          him. Ruling over many nations and
          having obtained dominion over the
          whole world, I was minded to make
          the lives of my subjects
          continually tranquil, desiring both
          to maintain the kingdom quiet and
          orderly to its utmost limits.
                    (MORE)

                    SCRIBE (V.O.) (CONT'D)
          Haman, who excels in soundness of
          judgment among us, informed us that
          a certain ill-disposed people is
          mixed up with all the tribes
          throughout the world, opposed in
          their law to every other nation,
          and continually neglecting the
          commands of the king, so that the
          united government blamelessly
          administered by us is not quietly
          established. Having then conceived
          that this nation alone of all
          others is continually set in
          opposition to every man,
          introducing as a change a foreign
          code of laws, and injuriously
          plotting to accomplish the worst of
          evils against our interests, and
          against the happy establishment of
          the monarchy; we signified to you
          in the letter written by Haman, to
          destroy them all utterly with their
          wives and children by the swords of
          the enemies, without pitying or
          sparing any, on the fourteenth day
          of the twelfth month Adar, of the
          present year.

EXT. THE KING'S PATIO - DUSK

As the sun sets on another beautiful day, King Ahasuerus and
Haman are sitting down having celebratory drink.

                    HAMAN
          It is good what we have done my
          king.

                    KING AHASUERUS
          I trust you Haman. If you say it is
          good, then it is good.

INT. MORDECAI'S HOME - NIGHT

Mordecai tears his clothes and places ash on his head.

Adina is crying as Mordecai runs from the home and through
the city streets.

EXT. SHUSHAN CITY STREETS - NIGHT

Mordecai, his clothes in tatters, runs through the streets.

He passes the Courtyard of the Women on his way to the king's gate.

He does not enter the gate but falls to his knees crying.

EXT. A BALCONY OVERLOOKING THE WOMAN'S COURTYARD - NIGHT

One of queen Esther's maids witnesses Mordecai running past and crying. She watches as he runs to the gates.

The maid tells Hathach.

EXT. KING'S GATE

Hathach stands inside the gate and watches Mordecai.

When Mordecai sees Hathach he walks to him and hands him a copy of the written decree.

Hathach tries to give Mordecai new clothes but he will not accept them.

Hathach returns to the citadel.

INT. ESTHER'S ROOM - NIGHT

Hathach and the maid who saw Mordecai enter the room.

Esther has been prepared for bed and is sitting with a few of her maid servants.

Both Hathach and the maid stand at the door. The maid stares at the floor.

Hathach with clinched jaw is very tense.

Esther notices Hathach and the maid at the door and beckons them to come in. She is confused by their apprehension to enter and approach her. <u>She is unaware of the decree.</u>

> ESTHER
> You two, come in. What is troubling
> you?

The two enter the room slowly.

> HATHACH
> My queen, the news grows more
> troubling.

Hathach hands Esther a copy of the decree which he received from Mordecai.

She unrolls it and reads while the others watch quietly.

As she reads, she does her best to hide her emotions.

                    ESTHER
          I must speak with Mordecai at once.

                    HATHACH
          But my queen he is a Jew...

Esther looks up at him. Her expression tells him that she already knows about Mordecai.

It suddenly dawns on Hathach that Esther is also a Jew.

                    HATHACH
          Come. I was planning to meet him at
          the courtyard gate.

                    ESTHER
          Thank you.

EXT. OUTER COURT OF THE HOUSE OF THE WOMEN - NIGHT

Hathach leads Esther to where Mordecai is waiting at the gate to the courtyard. She is covered in a hooded robe.

When they greet, they hug as father and daughter, something they have not been able to do for over a year now.

Hathach stands watch.

                    MORDECAI
          My daughter these are dangerous
          times. Why did you come to meet me
          yourself?

                    ESTHER
          I do not know what you expect me to
          do.

                    MORDECAI
          You must go to the king at once.

                    ESTHER
          You know that any man or woman who
          goes into the inner court to the
          king, who has not been called, he
          has but one law: put all to death.
                         (MORE)

                    ESTHER (CONT'D)
Only the one to whom the king holds
out the golden scepter will be
spared. Yet I myself have not been
called to go in to the king these
thirty days.

                    MORDECAI
Do not think in your heart that you
will escape in the king's palace
any more than all the other Jews.

                    ESTHER
I don't, but father...

                    MORDECAI
For if you remain completely silent
at this time, relief and
deliverance will arise for the Jews
from another place, but you and
your father's house will perish.
Yet who knows whether you have come
to the kingdom for *such* a time as
this?

                    ESTHER
Go, then. Gather all the Jews who
are present in Shushan, and fast
for me; neither eat nor drink for
three days, night or day. My maids
and I will fast likewise. And so I
will go to the king, which is
against the law; and if I perish, I
perish!

                    MORDECAI
My lovely Hadassah. I shall do as
you request. May the Lord
strengthen you with might and
wisdom.

The two hug and kiss again and Mordecai turns to leave.

Hathach takes Esther by the elbow and leads her away.

                    HATHACH
Esther, this man is your father?

                    ESTHER
Yes.

                    HATHACH
Then...you are...?

ESTHER
Yes. Hathach, can I trust you with
my secret? My life, and that of my
people, are in danger now.

The two walk in silence back to Esther's room.

MONTAGE - EXT. SHUSHAN CITY STREETS - NIGHT

Mordecai goes door to door to the Jewish homes. He knocks and
we see him talking the people who answer MOS.

At each home, the ones who answer the door nod in agreement
with what Mordecai is asking them to do.

INT. ESTHER'S ROOM - NIGHT

Esther has returned to her room.

Her maid servants are distraught by what is happening even
though most do not fully comprehend what that is.

HATHACH
My queen, what you have told
Mordecai you will do is certain
death. I cannot...

ESTHER
You cannot stop me. You are my
friend and have become my
confidant. I am trusting you to
support me during this time.

HATHACH
What would you have me do?

ESTHER
Stand guard at my door these next
three days. I shall entertain no
guests. Nor allow any food to be
brought to my quarters.

HATHACH
But...

ESTHER
Let it be as I request.

HATHACH
As you wish.

Hathach departs and closes the door to the Esther's room.

Once Hathach leaves the room, Esther finally allows her emotions to show. She breaks down and sobs openly before her maids. She falls to her knees and tears her clothes.

> ESTHER
> Come, help me out of these fine robes. I shall not adorn them again until I am prepared to meet my king.

The maids help her out of her robes and Esther pours ash from a cistern onto her head.

The maids do not know how to react. Some are crying. Others are scared.

EXT. KING'S GARDEN - DAY

Haman and Zeresh are walking through the king's garden.

Haman is pointing to various trees.

> HAMAN
> That one? Will that one do?

> ZERESH
> I think not.

Haman points to another. It would appear they have been doing this for some time in the hot midday sun.

Haman is growing impatient.

> HAMAN
> That one?

> ZERESH
> We must find the perfect tree and the perfect placement for the gallows that will hang the man who offended my husband.

> HAMAN
> I agree, but we run out of trees in this garden. Is not one suitable?

> ZERESH
> Haman, you have waited generations for your retribution, a few more minutes of looking will do you no harm.

                    HAMAN
        This, how about this fine specimen?

                    ZERESH
            No.

The obvious impatience can be seen all over Haman as he hangs
his shoulders. The two walk on in silence looking at the
various trees in the garden.

Finally, they come to a thorn tree, which stands tall.

Haman walks over to it and positions himself next to the tree
for scale reference.

                    HAMAN
        How about this tree my dear. It
        appears to be the proper height.

Zeresh studies the tree for a moment then smiles.

                    ZERESH
        I believe your torture is over my
        husband. Our search is finished.

                    HAMAN
        Finally.

Haman pats the trunk of the tree as if congratulating it for
being selected.

In doing so he inadvertently pricks his finger on one of the
thorns. He begins to bleed.

                    ZERESH
        Careful my dear.

                    HAMAN
        Even the tree which shall become
        Mordecai's gallows defies me.

                    ZERESH
        Come, let us begin the preparations
        and set the men to the
        construction.

INT. MORDECAI'S HOME - DAY

Mordecai is covered in ash and is wearing clothes of
mourning. He and Adina are on their knees in prayer.

                    MORDECAI
        Lord God, king ruling over all, all
        things are in your power, and there
        is no one that shall oppose you.
        You know, Lord, that it is not in
        insolence, nor haughtiness, nor
        love of glory, that I have done
        this, to refuse obeisance to the
        haughty Haman. For I would gladly
        have kissed the soles of his feet
        for the safety of Israel. But I
        have done this, that I might not
        set the glory of man above the
        glory of God: and I will not
        worship any one except you, my
        Lord. And now, O Lord God, the God
        of Abraham, spare your people, for
        our enemies are looking upon us to
        our destruction. Do not overlook
        your peculiar people, whom you have
        redeemed for yourself out of the
        land of Egypt. Hearken to my prayer
        and turn our mourning into
        gladness, that we may live and sing
        praise to your name, O Lord; and do
        not utterly destroy the mouth of
        them that praise you.

EXT. KING'S GARDEN - DUSK

The day is nearly over and workers have been busy
constructing a gallows around the tree selected by Haman and
Zeresh.

Haman stands proudly before the rising gallows, gloating in
his creation.

                    HAMAN
        Soon, it will be a good day to die.

INT. BET HA-MIDRASH - DAY

Mordecai is leading the men in prayer in the synagogue.
Everyone, including Mordecai is still covered in ash and sack
cloth.

The doors to the room are kicked open and guards armed with
spears and swords enter immediately surrounding the crowd.

Haman enters the room. Dressed again from head to toe in
black with a large embroidered image of a pagan idol on his
tunic in red and gold thread. He is so smug.

He pushes his way past the students so that he can face
Mordecai.

As he speaks, he nearly spits his words in a whispered tone.

> HAMAN
> I will first massacre these, and
> then I will hang you Mordecai. I
> have already prepared a place for
> you.

Mordecai stands defiantly facing Haman and does not say a
word.

This alone is an affront to Haman, who had hoped for a
reaction. When none is forthcoming Haman turns and commands
the guards.

> HAMAN
> Take them all. But leave this man.
> Let him witness the work of his
> disobedience.

The guards roughly shackle the men, placing chains around the
necks, hands and feet.

As they as chained they are lead away.

EXT. BET HA-MIDRASH - DAY

As the men are being lead out of the synagogue, the women
that are passing by begin crying out.

They throw themselves on the ground and in some cases plead
with the guards to free the men.

The guards are rougher with the women than the men; kicking
the women out of the way as they march the men to the
dungeon.

From the top of the stairs, Haman watches with great pleasure
his handiwork.

INT. ESTHER'S ROOM - NIGHT

Esther is laying on her bed. She is dressed is sack cloth and
her hair is a mess of knots and ashes. She has no makeup on
and has been crying.

The room is dark, even for being day time.

Hathach enters the room and speaks in whispers to one of Esther's maid servants who then approaches Esther and whispers to her.

Upon hearing the news Esther cries out.

                    ESTHER
          Leave me. All of you leave me now.

All of the maids leave the room.

Hathach hesitates to leave.

                    ESTHER
          Even you Hathach. Guard my door.
          Let no one in. Not one.

Hathach bows and leaves, closing the door behind him.

Esther knells and places her face to the floor.

                    ESTHER
          O my Lord, you alone are our king:
          help me who am destitute, and have
          no helper but you, for my danger is
          near at hand. I have heard from my
          birth, in the tribe of my kindred
          that you, Lord, took Israel out of
          all the nations for a perpetual
          inheritance. O Lord, do not resign
          your scepter to them that are not,
          and let them not laugh at our fall,
          but turn their counsel, against
          themselves, and make an example of
          him who has begun to injure us.
          Remember us, O Lord, manifest
          yourself in the time of our
          affliction, and encourage me. Put
          harmonious speech into my mouth
          before the lion, and turn his heart
          to hate him that fights against us,
          to the utter destruction of him
          that consent with him. But deliver
          us by your hand. You know my
          necessity, for I abhor the symbol
          of my proud station, which is upon
          my head in the days of my splendor.
          O Lord God of Abraham, who has
          power over all, hearken to the
          voice of the desperate, and deliver
          us from the hand of them that
          devise mischief; and deliver me
          from my fear.

When Esther finishes her prayer. She wipes her tears away and
stands. There is a renewed strength in her.

>   ESTHER
>   (calling out)
>   Hathach! Bring me my maids.

INT. ESTHER'S ROOM - LATER

Esther's maids are dressing her. She has been cleaned of the
ash and her hair has been combed smooth.

Hathach enters.

>   HATHACH
>   My queen, I cannot allow you to do
>   what you are planning.

>   ESTHER
>   I must Hathach.

>   HATHACH
>   But it is most certain death. You
>   have not been summoned by the king.
>   There are rules.

>   ESTHER
>   I am dead either way.

EXT. SHUSHAN CITEDAL - SUNRISE

The sun is rising on Shushan.

Rain has come through the night and washed the city.

As the sun rises a cock crows and shutters of homes begin to
open as the city awakes.

INT. MORDECAI'S HOME - MORNING

We see Mordecai and Adina in deep prayer.

INT. THE THRONE ROOM - DAY

The throne room is filled with scribes, officials, and
princes.

King Ahasuerus sits on his thrown.

Near him sits Haman in his place of authority.

The room is filled with THE BUZZ of daily activity.

Ahasuerus is in whispered conversation with one of his attendants MOS.

The huge three story tall doors to the throne room are swung open. As they slide open, slowly a throng of people begin to enter and exit.

KING'S PERSPECTIVE

Esther is standing in the inner courtyard. She is dressed in a lovely gown and her hair and make up are freshly done. She looks more lovely then the day of her wedding to the king

The king can only catch glimpses of her as the mass of people keep blocking his view.

He stands to make sure he has seen what he believes he has seen.

REVERSE ANGLE

Esther stands motionless in the inner courtyard. She can see the king as he stands and tries to look out and see her.

INT. THE THRONE ROOM

The king raises his hand for the room to quiet and it immediately does.

As the room quiets they all turn to see what it is that the king is looking at.

<u>We cannot tell if the king is angered or pleased by Esther's appearance.</u>

>   HAMAN
>   Was the queen called for, my king?

Ahasuerus waves Haman away.

Ahasuerus looks out at his queen.

The sun is entering the courtyard and is painting Esther in a beautiful light. She begins to radiate as if glowing and her dress sparkles in the sunlight.

Esther walks forward into the throne room even though she has not been called for.

Esther trembles from stress.

Though she appears cheerful, she strains with the fear in her heart.

Esther passes through the doors into the throne room as she approaches the king.

Ahasuerus is standing before his throne. He looks imposing, dressed in all his glorious apparel.

He looks with intense anger upon Esther and she falls to her knees. The color of her face goes ashen.

> HAMAN
> Guards! Arrest her at once!

The court echoes the CALL for the guards and for her punishment.

Esther regains her footing and stands perfectly still and quiet, not protesting or moving as she is forcibly grabbed and dragged before the king.

She is thrown down at his feet to receive his judgment and punishment.

The SHOUTING continues as the King looks down at his lovely queen. A spirit of gentleness sweeps over him.

Ahasuerus stands over the queen who he loves and holds out the golden scepter which grants her grace and permission to speak.

Esther raises her head and touches the top of the scepter, thus ensuring her safety.

The SHOUTING stops.

Haman looks on perturbed.

> KING AHASUERUS
> What is the matter, Esther? Be of
> good cheer, you shall not die, for
> our command is openly declared to
> you.

Having raised the golden scepter he lays it upon her neck and he embraces her.

> KING AHASUERUS
> Speak to me.

                    ESTHER
          I saw you, my lord, as an angel of
          God, and my heart was troubled for
          fear of your glory; for you, my
          lord, art to be wondered at, and
          your face is full of grace.

While she is speaking, she grows faint again in his arms.

Ahasuerus is troubled by this and calls for his servants to comforted her.

Ahasuerus returns to his throne as the attendants see to Esther.

When she regains her strength she rises and bows in respect to the king.

All eyes are on her.

                KING AHASUERUS
          What do you wish, Queen Esther?
          What is your request? It shall be
          given to you -- up to half the
          kingdom!

                    ESTHER
          If it pleases the king, let the
          king and Haman come today to the
          banquet that I have prepared for
          him.

                KING AHASUERUS
          Is that all?

Esther bows deeply.

                    ESTHER
          Yes my king.

Ahasuerus smiles and turns to Haman.

<u>Haman's mood has changed now because of the request.</u> He nods acknowledgment of his approval to the king.

                KING AHASUERUS
          So let it be done. We shall come to
          you as the sun sets this day for a
          feast you have prepared for us.

                    ESTHER
          Thank you my king. You and Haman
          honor me.

EXT. WOMEN'S GARDEN - LATE AFTERNOON

The sun is setting on Shushan.

The garden is decorated even more beautifully than it
naturally is. Candles and cisterns are burning around the
area and a table set for two is made up in royal decor.
Flowers and fruits line the table and a large vessel for wine
and two goblets sit on the table.

Ahasuerus and Haman enter the courtyard preceded by the
king's guards. They both take in the lush beauty of the
setting and proceed to sit at the table.

Esther enters the court followed by Hathach and her two maids
that were with her earlier.

She serves both Ahasuerus and Haman wine and places fruit on
their plates.

> KING AHASUERUS
> To what do we deserve this honor my
> queen?

> ESTHER
> I have missed my king and I simply
> wish to bless him and his trusted
> advisor.

Esther looks at Haman, who smiles and tips his goblet of wine
to her, acknowledging the compliment.

> KING AHASUERUS
> It has been very busy times of
> late. I apologize that we have not
> seen more of each other.

> ESTHER
> Your presence here tonight erases
> all of the past days and nights
> without you.

> KING AHASUERUS
> Surely you have some petition. What
> is it? It shall be granted you.

Esther's hand shakes as she pours more wine for Ahasuerus.

She nearly drops the vessel into his lap.

He reaches out and grabs the vessel and takes her hand in
his.

Hathach reacts as well from a distance, but stays back.

                    KING AHASUERUS
          What is it my queen? You are
          trembling like a leaf.

                    ESTHER
          All pardons my king.

                    KING AHASUERUS
          Are you ill?

                    ESTHER
          No my king.

                    KING AHASUERUS
          Sit. Enjoy some of this banquet you
          have prepared for us, and let the
          maids serve you.

                    ESTHER
          Thank you, no. I wish to serve you
          tonight. But please, if it pleases
          the king allow me to go and gather
          myself.

                    KING AHASUERUS
          Of course.

Esther excuses herself.

Ahasuerus and Haman continued to feast and drink.

                    KING AHASUERUS
          She seems so frail tonight. I have
          not seen her like this before.

                    HAMAN
          It would appear that something does
          trouble the queen.

                    KING AHASUERUS
          Yes.
              (pausing)
          Have you heard of anything that may
          have occurred which would trouble
          her?

                    HAMAN
          No my king.

Ahasuerus sits pensively.

Soon Esther enters again. She seems more composed now.

                    KING AHASUERUS
          Are you feeling better my queen?

                    ESTHER
          Yes much. Thank you. Is the food
          and drink to your liking?

                    KING AHASUERUS
          Yes, very much.

                    ESTHER
          And Haman?

                    HAMAN
          Yes my queen. You honor me with the
          invitation.

Esther smiles.

                    KING AHASUERUS
          Now come. For you to have risked
          your life earlier, there must be
          some petition you have for me?

                    ESTHER
          If there is one my king, it is
          this: if I have found favor in the
          sight of the king, and if it
          pleases the king to grant my
          petition and fulfill my request,
          then let the king and Haman come to
          the banquet which I will prepare
          for them, and tomorrow I will do as
          the king has said.

Ahasuerus and Haman look across the table at each other
confused but also delighted at the thought of enjoying
another fine meal as this.

Ahasuerus laughs a hearty laugh and smiles, taking Esther's
hands in his again.

                    KING AHASUERUS
          It would be my delight to return
          again tomorrow. Haman? Will you
          join us again?

                    HAMAN
          Of course my king. I would be
          doubly honored.

Esther smiles and bows. The maid servants bring more food for
the king and Haman.

EXT. KING'S GATE - NIGHT

Haman is leaving the palace after the wonderful feast with
the king and Esther. He walks along as if he owns the place.
A large smile on his face. He struts like a peacock, full of
pride.

He nears the King's gate where he sees Mordecai and the
Sanhedrin still sitting and talking in hushed tones to each
other MOS.

The crowds have thinned for the day with most people having
returned home for dinner.

The Sanhedrin all cower before Haman as he walks past but
Mordecai sits tall in his seat defiantly, and stares directly
at Haman.

The two lock eyes. These men hate each other with every fiber
of their person.

Haman marches home. His joy now lost. Now as he walks, he
stomps and sulks.

INT. HAMAM'S HOME - NIGHT

Haman slams the door as he enters. The main room is filled
with Haman's closest friends and Zeresh. Across the table are
astrological charts.

Sensing Haman's mood and trying to diffuse the situation
because they have guests, Zeresh approaches Haman quickly and
tries to comfort him.

                    ZERESH
          Haman, I have invited your friends
          to celebrate the honor that Queen
          Esther bestowed on your with her
          invitation tonight.

                    HAMAN
          I am in no mood woman.

                    COUNSELOR
          What is it that bothers you? Was
          the banquet not wonderful?

                    HAMAN
          The banquet was exceptional. In
          fact I have been invited to another
          tomorrow by the queen.

                    COUNSELOR
          Then why the foul mood?

                    HAMAN
          It is this Mordecai.

                    COUNSELOR
          Haman, this man means nothing. He
          is less than nothing.

                    COUNSELOR 2
          Yes, and soon he shall be dead, by
          your own decree.

                    COUNSELOR
          Why let him torment you so?

Haman slams his hand on the table. The noise startles
everyone in the room.

Zeresh places her hands on his shoulder to comfort him.

                    HAMAN
          He does! His very existence is like
          hot coals on my skin.

                    ZERESH
          But soon he shall swing from the
          gallows you have built just for
          him.

Haman calms at the touch and words of his wife.

                    ZERESH
          There is no one that can defy the
          great Haman. Even the king himself
          listens to your counsel and does
          not question it.

                    HAMAN
          You speak truth.

                    ZERESH
          You are greatly to be honored.

                    COUNSELOR
          Yes, Haman, your name is known
          throughout all the land.

                    COUNSELOR 2
          Even the queen has honored you.
          Twice in two days.

Haman's pride is beginning to return. He stands taller and a confidence sweeps over him.

> HAMAN
> Besides, Queen Esther invited no one but me to come in with the king.

> ZERESH
> There you see.

> HAMAN
> Yet all this avails me nothing, so long as I see Mordecai the Jew sitting at the king's gate.

> ZERESH
> In the morning suggest to the king that Mordecai be hanged; then go merrily with the king to the banquet.

Haman smiles as the group of counselors all nod in agreement.

INT. ESTHER'S ROOM - NIGHT

Esther is is preparing for bed.

She looks tired, _from carrying the burden of her task_, but in good spirits.

There is a knock at the door.

Hathach answers and allows Hegai to enter.

Hegai bows before Esther.

> HEGAI
> My queen, I have completed the task on which you sent me.

> ESTHER
> Were there any problems?

> HEGAI
> No my queen. It is all prepared as you have requested.

> ESTHER
> You have always been a good friend. Thank you.

                    HEGAI
          It is I that should thank you. You
          have brought much light to the
          king's heart and this palace.

Hegai leaves.

                    HATHACH
          My queen, if I may speak plainly?

                    ESTHER
          Of course.

                    HATHACH
          This is a dangerous intrigue you
          are involved in.

                    ESTHER
          I did not chose this time, it
          choose me.

                    HATHACH
          I just wish for your safety.

                    ESTHER
          Then help me, as you have done.
          Soon, the truth shall be known on
          all accounts.

                    HATHACH
          I am always at your service my
          queen.

Esther smiles and Hathach leaves to his position at the door.

The maids help Esther to her bed.

INT. THE KING'S CHAMBERS - NIGHT

The king is prepared for sleep as well, but he is restless.
He paces his room. One of the attendants is with the king.

                    ATTENDANT
          My king is there something that
          will sooth your mind? Maybe you
          would like to hear the record of
          your chronicles be read to you?

                    KING AHASUERUS
          Yes. That would be good. Have it
          done.

The attendant goes to collect a scroll from a pile that is on the king's table. He sorts through them obviously looking for a very specific scroll.

He returns to the king who has now laid down in his bed. The attendant stands as he reads.

> ATTENDANT
> On this day of our King Ahasuerus, in the third year of his reign, it was made known about the plot of Bigthana and Teresh, two of the king's eunuchs and doorkeepers, that they have plotted to lay hands on the king to his destruction.

> KING AHASUERUS
> I remember this event. Continue.

> ATTENDANT
> The plot of Bigthana and Teresh was made known to the king by his Queen Esther. The queen requested of King Ahasuerus that all honor be bestowed on one Mordecai whom brought the matter to the queen's attention.

> KING AHASUERUS
> What honor or dignity has been bestowed on Mordecai for this?

The attendant looks through the scroll.

> ATTENDANT
> It would appear, my king, that nothing has been done for him.

The king sits up in his bed.

> KING AHASUERUS
> Nothing?

> ATTENDANT
> There is nothing recorded that he has been honored.

> KING AHASUERUS
> A man saves the king's life and he is not honored in any manner?
> (MORE)

                    KING AHASUERUS (CONT'D)
          Make note, first thing in the
          morning, whoever is first in the
          court, I want them to be allowed
          entrance so that they can make
          haste to honor this Mordecai.

                    ATTENDANT
          As you wish my king. It shall be
          done.

                    KING AHASUERUS
          Leave me now.

The attendant backs out of the room.

INT. HALL OUTSIDE OF THE KING'S CHAMBERS

Hegai greets the attendant. No words are exchanged but the
attendant nods to Hegai in acknowledgment that the task was
completed.

INT. HAMAM'S HOME - MORNING

Haman is preparing to leave for the king's court. He is
dressed in fine clothes. Zeresh is with him.

                    HAMAN
          Today, I shall finally have my
          revenge on Mordecai.

                    ZERESH
          The time for your plan against the
          Jews and for this Mordecai are
          nearly upon us.

                    HAMAN
          Yes. It feels good and right.
          Finally, to be free of this
          torment.

                    ZERESH
          How will ask the king?

                    HAMAN
          I will simply explain to him how
          Mordecai continues to lead the Jews
          in disobedience against the king's
          decrees.

                    ZERESH
          The king will not tolerate that.

> HAMAN
> Exactly. He will order Mordecai
> hanged at once.

> ZERESH
> And you will have the gallows
> already prepared.

> HAMAN
> It is a glorious day.

INT. THE THRONE ROOM - DAY

The king sits on his throne. Only a few of his attendants and
scribes are in the hall with him.

The door to the hall is open and Haman struts in.

The king looks up and notices Haman as soon as he enters.

> KING AHASUERUS
> Ah Haman. I am glad you are here.

The attendant hurries off to take care of whatever the king
has previously been discussing with him.

> HAMAN
> Thank you, my king. I have a
> petition to make of you.

> KING AHASUERUS
> That is fine, but first, it has
> come to my attention that I have
> failed to pay honor to a very
> important man in this kingdom.

> HAMAN
> Really?

Haman stands a bit taller as he continues to walk to his
place beside the king.

He sits in his chair.

> KING AHASUERUS
> What shall be done for the man whom
> the king delights to honor?

Haman smiles, he believes the king is talking about him.

                    HAMAN
          For the man whom the king delights
          to honor, let a royal robe be
          brought which the king has worn,
          and a horse on which the king has
          ridden, which has a royal crest
          placed on its head. Then let this
          robe and horse be delivered to the
          hand of one of the king's most
          noble princes, that he may array
          the man whom the king delights to
          honor. Then parade him on horseback
          through the city square, and
          proclaim before him: 'Thus shall it
          be done to the man whom the king
          delights to honor!'

Ahasuerus thinks about what Haman has proposed.

                    KING AHASUERUS
          You think it will be honor enough?

Haman smiles a wide smile. He is so proud of himself.

                    HAMAN
          Yes, my king. Any man would be more
          than honored to be bestowed with
          this offering.

                    KING AHASUERUS
          Hurry then, take the robe and the
          horse, as you have suggested, and
          do so for Mordecai! Leave nothing
          undone of all that you have spoken.

Haman's face drops and his entire countenance changes with
the king's words. He cannot believe his ears.

                    HAMAN
          My king?

                    KING AHASUERUS
          You heard me. Mordecai. The man who
          saved my life. He has yet to be
          honored and I wish for you to do as
          you have rightly suggested. You
          have much good counsel Haman. Now
          go.

                    HAMAN
          Yes my king.

Haman stands to leave. The swaggered he had when walking into the throne room is all but vanished. In is place is utter defeat and disgust.

> KING AHASUERUS
> Oh Haman, what was your petition
> you wished to make?

Haman turns to face the king but can barely speak now, he is so filled with anger.

> HAMAN
> Another time my king.

> KING AHASUERUS
> Very well. Hurry now.

EXT. KING'S GATE - DAY

Mordecai is sitting with the Sanhedrin in their normal place inside the king's gate.

A guard approaches Mordecai.

> GUARD
> Mordecai?

> MORDECAI
> Yes.

> GUARD
> Please come with me.

> MORDECAI
> May I inquire as to where we are
> going?

> GUARD
> I have been told to fetch you for
> the king. Honor is to bestowed upon
> you for your service to him.

Mordecai smiles a wary smile and the Sanhedrin pat him on the back with congratulations.

INT. KING'S STABLES - DAY

Haman is standing in the royal stables. He has had prepared a royal stallion. The horse is regally attired with the king's crest on its head.

Haman stands waiting for Mordecai who is ushered into the stables by the guards.

Mordecai is surprised to see Haman standing there and even more surprised when Haman places one of the king's royal robes around his shoulders.

>   HAMAN
>   Mordecai, it is the king's pleasure
>   to honor you today for your service
>   in saving his life.

Haman turns and motions for the guards to help Mordecai up onto the horse.

He then takes the reigns of the beautiful horse and begins to lead Mordecai out into the streets of Shushan.

EXT. SHUSHAN CITY STREETS - DAY

Haman is leading Mordecai, who is sitting tall in the saddle of the royal horse, through the streets. As he leads the way, Haman proclaims over and over:

>   HAMAN
>   (repeatedly)
>   Thus shall it be done to the man
>   whom the king delights to honor!

INT. ESTHER'S ROOM - DAY

Hathach enters Esther's room.

>   HATHACH
>   Esther, come. You must witness what
>   is taking place in the streets.

Esther runs to the window with her maid servants.

They look out to see the scene of Haman marching Mordecai through the streets.

Mordecai looks up to see Esther standing at her window. He smiles to her and she to him.

Haman notices this small exchanged.

When Esther see Haman looking at her, she turns back into her room.

>   HATHACH
>   This is good.

                    ESTHER
          Yes. But I fear this will only
          exasperate the matter.

                    HATHACH
          The feast is tonight for the king.
          Will you tell the king your plight?

                    ESTHER
          Tonight is my night of destiny.

EXT. KING'S GATE - DAY

Mordecai is returned to the gate.

His friends all greet him and congratulate him again. He is
basking in his glory and honor.

Haman on the other hand sulks as he fades off into the crowd.
He covers his head so no one can recognize him.

INT. HAMAM'S HOME - DAY

Haman enters his home and slams the door.

He drops down into a chair and covers his head and weeps.

Zeresh enters the room.

                    ZERESH
          What is it that troubles you now my
          husband?

                    MORDECAI
          It is this Mordecai, again! It is
          as if he has been sent to be a
          torment to me. A curse.

                    ZERESH
          Is he not to be hanged?

                    HAMAN
          I was not able to make my petition
          known to the king. Instead, today
          I had to honor Mordecai with the
          king's robe and a procession
          through the city.

                    ZERESH
          How did this come to be?

                    HAMAN
          Before I could make my request
          before the king, he asked me how I
          would honor a man that the king was
          well pleased with. I thought he was
          talking about me. How was I to know
          he would honor a man such as
          Mordecai.

Zeresh walks around the room. She has a look of great concern
on her face now as she paces.

                    HAMAN
          The king is unaware that Mordecai
          is a Jew.

                    ZERESH
          Fear troubles me deeply Haman. I
          feel an ill omen has settled upon
          you.

                    HAMAN
          What? What are you saying?

Zeresh continues to pace.

                    HAMAN
          Woman! Stop that pacing and answer
          me!

                    ZERESH
          I fear that Mordecai, before whom
          you have begun to fall, you will
          not prevail against him.

                    HAMAN
          No! The decree is set. Mordecai and
          the rest of the Jews are set for
          utter destruction. And...

                    ZERESH
          What?

                    HAMAN
          Today, when we passed the Queen's
          quarters, I noticed Mordecai
          looking up Esther. There seems to
          be a connection between those two.

                    ZERESH
          So.

                    HAMAN
          What do we know of this Esther?
          Where she came from? Who are her
          parents?

A look of understanding crosses Zeresh's face.

                    HAMAN
          What if the Queen is Jewish? She
          will have lied to the king.
          Tonight, at her banquet I shall
          question her in front of the king.

                    ZERESH
          This is a dangerous intrigue Haman.
          Even for you. I fear it shall not
          go well for you.

                    HAMAN
          Stop saying that woman!

Haman slaps Zeresh across the face.

She falls to the floor, only to look up at Haman in total
disgust.

She stands, a strong defiant woman and leaves the room.

INT. QUEEN ESTHER'S HALL - NIGHT

What was once Queen Vashti's hall is now Esther's. The room
has been redecorated to suit Esther's taste. While still
opulent it is more humble and sedate.

A table is set with a feast even larger than the previous
night's.

When King Ahasuerus and Haman enter the room, Esther and her
entourage are already standing at attention at the other end.

They bow to the king and Haman as the two men enter followed
by their guards. Eunuchs usher the men to their seats.

Esther is even more lovely then the night before, if
possible. She is stunning to behold.

This banquet is more formal than the previous banquet and
Esther joins them at the table.

King Ahasuerus is seated at the head, Esther sits to his
right and Haman to his left directly across from Esther.

When they are seated Haman stares directly at Esther with hate filled eyes.

Esther, already nervous, looks away quickly.

> KING AHASUERUS
> You have outdone yourself Esther.
> This is a banquet suitable for all
> the princes of the provinces.

> ESTHER
> My king, you and Haman are more
> than worthy.

> KING AHASUERUS
> We thank you for the honor.

Ahasuerus notices that Haman is glaring at Esther.

> KING AHASUERUS
> Haman? Are we not honored by the
> queen's gesture.

> HAMAN
> Yes, my king. This is a wondrous
> banquet. Was this not Queen
> Vashti's hall?

> ESTHER
> Yes. I thought we would be more
> comfortable here tonight.

> HAMAN
> And to what do we deserve such
> honor my queen?

> KING AHASUERUS
> Are you not grateful?

> HAMAN
> Very much so, my king. One simply
> wonders why two banquets on two
> nights. What is the occasion?

Both men turn to look at Esther. She is noticeably nervous.

Hathach, in the background looks like he is ready to tear Haman's head off.

> KING AHASUERUS
> This is a wonderful feast you have
> prepared Esther. What is your
> petition? It shall be granted you.

Esther bows to her king.

                    ESTHER
          Before I present my petition,
          please let us enjoy some of this
          feast.

                    KING AHASUERUS
          As you wish.

Esther pours wine for Ahasuerus and Haman.

Haman continues to stare at her and watches her every move.

The maids move to the table and begin to present each with
some of the lush fruits and meats to chose from.

As the three start to enjoy their meal Haman asks Esther:

                    HAMAN
          My Queen, please tell me about your
          history and family. I fear I do not
          know as much as I would like about
          where you are from.

Esther is surprised and completely unprepared for such a
direct question.

Ahasuerus looks up from his food curious and somewhat amused.

                    KING AHASUERUS
          I also would love to learn more
          about the woman who has captured my
          heart.

                    ESTHER
          As you know I am from Susa. I have
          lived here most of my life.

                    HAMAN
          Oh, is your family still alive?

                    ESTHER
          Yes.

                    HAMAN
          Do they reside in Susa as well?

                    ESTHER
          Yes.

                    KING AHASUERUS
          Esther, I have never meet your
          family.
                         (MORE)

                    KING AHASUERUS (CONT'D)
          I was not aware they lived here.
          Why have you not brought them to
          the palace?

                    HAMAN
          Yes, why have we never met the
          family of our queen? You are not
          ashamed of them are you?

                    ESTHER
          Never.

                    KING AHASUERUS
          We should send for them.

                    HAMAN
          Yes. This banquet is large enough
          for many more.

                    ESTHER
          My lords, tonight is meant to be a
          night to honor you both, I do not
          wish to distract from that.

                    HAMAN
          I for one would be honored to meet
          the family of our queen.

                    KING AHASUERUS
          Yes. Let it be done. Esther, let
          the guards call on your family and
          bring them her.

                    ESTHER
          But the hour is late.

Ahasuerus is growing impatient.

Haman is pleased with himself.

                    KING AHASUERUS
          Nonsense. It is never too late to
          do as the king commands.

Esther is in a panic. She looks over her shoulders to Hathach
who can only look at her with a sympathetic look.

                    KING AHASUERUS
          Esther, tell the guards, where your
          family lives and let them be
          brought here at once.

Esther sits in silence. She looks down at her hands.

                    KING AHASUERUS
          Esther! I will not be ignored.

                    ESTHER
          If I have found favor in your
          sight, O king, and if it pleases
          the king, let my life be given me
          at my petition, and my people at my
          request.

                    KING AHASUERUS
          What?

                    HAMAN
          Now she makes her petition? What is
          the queen hiding?

                    ESTHER
          My king?

Esther looks at Ahasuerus with pleading eyes. <u>She has always
found favor with him and tonight is no different.</u>

                    KING AHASUERUS
          What is your petition? It shall be
          granted you.

                    ESTHER
          My family, my people and I, we have
          been sold to be destroyed, to be
          killed, and to be annihilated. Had
          we been sold as male and female
          slaves, I would have held my
          tongue, although the enemy could
          never compensate for the king's
          loss.

                    HAMAN
          What people? You will not even
          tells us who your family is?

A boldness comes over Esther and she stands.

                    ESTHER
          My people are the Jews. My name is
          Hadassah, I am the daughter of
          Mordecai, who was honored this day
          by my king.

Haman stands.

                    HAMAN
          A Jew! My king, were you aware of
          this?

Ahasuerus is sitting at the table lost in thought at the news.

> HAMAN
> How could you withhold this information from the king? You have lied about who you are to gain this position. Guards!

The guards enter the room and approach Esther to take her.

Hathach steps in the way and fights with one of them before he can lay hands on Esther.

Esther kneels before the king and rests her head on his feet.

> ESTHER
> My king. I love you. Do not let the one who has sold me and my people succeed.

> KING AHASUERUS
> Who is he? Where is he? Who would dare presume in his heart to do such a thing?

Esther lifts her head and points to Haman.

> ESTHER
> The adversary and enemy is this wicked Haman!

Ahasuerus turns to Haman who backs away from the table with a look of terror on his face.

Ahasuerus stands to confront Him.

Hathach pushes the guards away from Esther who stands and goes to the windows.

She tears down the drapes to reveal the palace gardens below where the gallows that Haman had built are located.

Hegai and other eunuchs are standing near it with torches so it can be seen in the dark.

> ESTHER
> My king, Haman has already constructed a gallows on which he was determined to hang the very man who saved your life.

Haman is backing away from the king but the guards are blocking the exit from the hall.

                  HAMAN
        My king. I was unaware you wished
        to honor Mordecai. I did not even
        know he was a Jew. But you have
        established a decree.

Ahasuerus steps toward Haman.

               KING AHASUERUS
        I have been betrayed here tonight.

               HAMAN
        Yes! Yes, that is what I have
        attempted to show you.

               KING AHASUERUS
        But not by my queen and wife.

               HAMAN
        My king?

               KING AHASUERUS
        You Haman. You have plotted to
        deceive me and to destroy the very
        people who have done nothing but
        bring peace and love to my life.

Haman, in an act of desperation grabs one of the guard's
swords and races to Esther to attack her.

Hathach stops him with a powerful blow which drops him to the
floor.

               KING AHASUERUS
        Will you also assault the queen
        while I am in the house? Guards!

The guards cover Haman's face and carry him away.

               KING AHASUERUS
        Hang him on the very gallows he
        built!

Haman is carried from the room SCREAMING.

Ahasuerus turns to Esther who stands humbly before him.

               ESTHER
        I am sorry my king. I never meant
        to deceive you.

               KING AHASUERUS
        Hush. There is no deception if the
        question was never asked.
               (MORE)

> KING AHASUERUS (CONT'D)
> You are your family have honored me
> again and again. For this I love
> you.

> ESTHER
> And I love you.

Ahasuerus takes Esther into his arms and they kiss.

Esther is crying.

> KING AHASUERUS
> My queen why do you still cry?

> ESTHER
> If it pleases the king, let it be
> written to revoke the letters
> devised by Haman. For how can I
> endure to see the evil that will
> come to my people? Or how can I
> endure to see the destruction of my
> countrymen?

> KING AHASUERUS
> It shall be done as you say. Do not
> worry my queen, I shall not lose
> you or allow any harm to befall on
> you.

INT. THE THRONE ROOM - DAY

The room is filled as it has been on many occasion with the
princes of the provinces, the scribes, attendants and many
from the city.

Esther sits in her place at the right hand of the king as he
presides over the court.

The large doors at the end of the room are opened and
Mordecai is lead into the hall. He is ushered to the front of
the room and before the king.

Ahasuerus rises and steps down to meet Mordecai, who has
bowed before the king.

> KING AHASUERUS
> Rise Mordecai. You are a friend to
> this king.

Mordecai rises and Ahasuerus hugs him.

Ahasuerus faces the crowd.

> KING AHASUERUS
> Indeed, this day, I have given
> Esther the house of Haman, and they
> have hanged him on the gallows
> because he tried to lay his hand on
> the Jews.

Mordecai was unaware of this and looks up to Esther who
smiles to him and nods.

> KING AHASUERUS
> Mordecai, you yourselves write a
> decree concerning the Jews, as you
> please, in the king's name, and
> seal it with the king's signet
> ring.

Ahasuerus removes his signet ring, which had previously been
given to Haman and hands it to Mordecai.

Mordecai is humbled and elated. He places the ring on his
finger.

> MORDECAI
> Nothing more my king. For on this
> day, we shall rest and hold a great
> feast -- the Feast of Purim.

> ESTHER
> Because of you my king this month
> has been turned from sorrow to joy.
> From mourning to a holiday.

> KING AHASUERUS
> Surely not I, but you Esther.

The crowd CHEERS.

Esther steps down to hug her father. There are tears in both
of their eyes. Tears of happiness.

The king's attendants place robes of blue and white around
Mordecai and place a great crown of gold upon his head.

He is arrayed in a garment of fine linen and purple and
ushered out of the throne room.

EXT. SHUSHAN CITY STREETS - DAY

The streets are filled with people CHEERING and joyful. There
is a royal procession with Mordecai as the honoree.

EXT. SUNRISE OVER SHUSHAN - MORNING

The grand vista of Shushan and the Persian desert.

TEXT FADES IN OVER THE SCENE. THE TEXT BEGINS IN HEBREW
LETTER AND TRANSFORMS TO ENGLISH.

"And Mordecai said, 'These things have been done of God. The
nations are those nations that combined to destroy the name
of the Jews. But as for my nation, this is Israel, even they
that cried to God and were delivered: for the Lord delivered
his people. And the Lord rescued us out of all these
calamities; and God wrought such signs and great wonders as
have not been done among the nations. And God remembered his
people, and vindicated his inheritance."

                                        FADE TO BLACK.

LOGLINE

After being crowned at local scholarship pageants, two young women, become friends as they vie for the state title and must help each other overcome personal issues if either stands a chance of winning the crown.

TOP FIVE

Written by

Douglas King

FADE IN:

INT. HIGH SCHOOL THEATER - NIGHT

ALYSSA ALVAREZ (20), the girl next door you always wanted to
be friends with, holds hands with KAREN (21), at center
stage. They wait to hear their name called as the winner of a
local pageant.

                    EMCEE (O.C.)
          And, the next Miss Allen is --

INT. COMMUNITY THEATER - NIGHT

MORGAN HARRISON (20), a stunning young woman who stands on
stage with more composure than most politicians, holds hands
with PARIS, (19). They wait to hear if their name is called
as the winner.

                    EMCEE 2 (O.C.)
          And our new Miss Highland Park is --

Morgan smiles at Paris. A comforting but self-assured smile,
as if to say, "you know I am the winner..."

BACK TO HIGH SCHOOL THEATER

The crowd cheers for both girls as they stand in the
spotlight.

                    EMCEE (O.C.)
          Contestant number seven, Alyssa
          Alvarez!

Never has someone been more surprised in their life. Karen
hugs Alyssa, who is still in shock as a crown is placed on
her head and a sash draped over her shoulder.

Alyssa waves at the audience with tears running down her
cheeks and a smile bright enough to power the city.

Her parents, CAMILlA and RAMON, stand and cheer in the
audience.

BACK TO COMMUNITY THEATER

The crowd cheers for Morgan and Paris as they stand on stage.

                    EMCEE 2 (O.C.)
              Contestant number 12, Morgan
              Harrison!

Morgan, gives a courteous hug to Paris, accepts the crown and
sash as if they were expected, and walks the stage. She owns
it.

She waves to the audience, thanks the judges, and smiles for
the cameras. All in a day's work for Morgan.

Her parents, JOANNE and ANTHONY, stand and cheer. Joanne
beams with pride.

The cheer of the crowd continues as...

INT. MORGAN'S PARENT HOME - BEDROOM - MORNING

...Sunlight enters Morgan's room, illuminating numerous
pageant trophies, tiaras, sashes and photos of Morgan being
crowned. All the items have been meticulously arranged as the
predominate decor of the room.

Morgan sleeps under a pile of blankets.

The door to her room bursts open as Joanne, a force to be
reckoned with, enters wearing fitness attire.

She opens the blinds, flooding the room with more light and
pulls the covers off the bed.

                    JOANNE
              Let's go, Sleeping Beauty. State is
              only nine months away. We've got to
              keep in shape if we expect to win
              this year.

Morgan buries her head under the sheets that remain covering
her.

                    MORGAN
              Mom!

                    JOANNE
              Let's keep the momentum going.

                    MORGAN
              I think I can take one day to bask
              in my glory.

                    JOANNE
          Please. You've known so much glory
          you barely acknowledge it, let
          alone bask in it. I'll be outside
          stretching. I expect to see you in
          five minutes.

Joanne exits as Morgan GROANS from under the sheet covering
her.

INT. ALYSSA'S BEDROOM - MORNING

It is as quiet as a church on Monday inside Alyssa's room. A
typical college-age student's room where Alyssa is in a deep,
coma like sleep.

Movement confirms that she is still part of the living.

INT. ALVAREZ'S KITCHEN - SAME

Camilla, the type of women who knows her way around a board
room as well as a kitchen, cooks bacon and pancakes while,
Ramon, the strong silent type, sits reading the paper.

Alyssa, slowly enters the room rubbing sleep from her eyes
and looking nothing like the pageant queen she was the night
before.

                    ALYSSA
          What's all this?

                    CAMILLA
          You've been dieting for weeks. Now
          you get to celebrate.

Ramon looks up from his paper, grabs a strip of bacon while
looking at the zombie that is his daughter.

                    RAMON
          If the judges saw you now they may
          not have given you the title.

Alyssa and Camilla slap him on opposing shoulders.

                    CAMILLA
          Be nice. You could be talking to
          the next representative for Texas.

                    RAMON
          More like, Miss Walking Dead.

                    ALYSSA
          Dad!? I just woke up.

                    RAMON
          From a one hundred year dirt nap?

                    CAMILLA
          Leave her be, or no more bacon for
          you.

Alyssa sits down at the table and her mom places a stack of
warm pancakes in front of her, butter and syrup dripping down
the sides.

                    CAMILLA (CONT'D)
          You earned a little rest.

Ramon, raises the paper to hide his face from Camilla but
looks to Alyssa.

                    RAMON
          I'm proud of you, little monkey.
          You're always the winner in my
          book.

Alyssa smiles until her dad steals one of her pieces of
bacon.

EXT. MORGAN'S PARENT'S HOME - DAY

Morgan and Joanne, run down the street and turn into their
driveway.

A car is parked there. Morgan recognizes the driver who gets
out of the car while texting on his phone.

                    MORGAN
          Tommy!

Morgan runs up and tries to hug her pageant director, TOMMY
FORD, who is the poster child for impeccable test. He shrinks
from her sweaty grasp.

                    TOMMY
          Oh no, girl. You have to towel off
          and spray some perfume before you
          get to hold this body.

                    MORGAN
          C'mon, it's just a little sweat.

                    TOMMY
          Honey, the only time I allow sweat
          near me is when I am sunning pool
          side. No. You get yourself inside
          and cleaned up. Then we can talk
          appearances. I have something for
          you already.

                    MORGAN
          Great. I'll be right back.

Morgan runs into the home. Joanne approaches Tommy and in a
more sophisticated manner, exchanges air hugs and kisses.

                    JOANNE
          Come in. I'll juice some kale.

                    TOMMY
          Unless, you're going to splash a
          lot of vodka in it, I'll pass.

                    JOANNE
          That can be arranged.

Joanne smiles as the two enter the home.

INT. MORGAN'S PARENT'S HOME - KITCHEN - SAME

A freshly toweled off Morgan, Joanne and Tommy sit around the
kitchen table.

Joanne has forced a glass of freshly made kale juice in front
of both Morgan and Tommy, who each grimace.

                    MORGAN
          So, what you got for me?

                    TOMMY
          Have you heard of Operation Care?

                    MORGAN
          No.

                    TOMMY
          It's a wonderful charity which is
          planning a major celebration for
          the homeless of DFW.

                    JOANNE
          We celebrate homeless now?

                    TOMMY
          They just call it that, dear. It's
          an event held at the convention
          center where they provide haircuts,
          make-overs, food, medical testing
          and more. There will be zip lines
          and rock walls for the kids. It's
          really amazing, all they do.

                    MORGAN
          Sounds awesome.

                    JOANNE
          And will look good for your
          community service hours.

                    MORGAN
          So what do I get to do? Dance? Sign
          photos?

                    TOMMY
          They want some of the girls to wash
          the feet of the homeless.

                    MORGAN
          Oh.

                    TOMMY
          It's a big part of their program.

                    JOANNE
          Remember, honey, one of the points
          of the crown is service.

                    MORGAN
          So there will be other contestants
          there as well?

                    TOMMY
          Yes. Some of the other directors
          and I wanted to bring as many girls
          as possible to support this
          organization.

Morgan thinks about it.

                    MORGAN
          Okay. Count me in.

EXT. DALLAS CONVENTION CENTER - MORNING

A long line of homeless people queue at the door waiting to
get in.

INT. DALLAS CONVENTION CENTER - CONTINUOUS

SUSIE JENNINGS, the founder of Operation Care, a dynamo of a woman who only stands a bit taller than five feet, greets a group of six local title holders behind curtains separating them from the event.

Morgan and Alyssa are there, standing a few feet away from each other.

Morgan glances over to check out Alyssa. Alyssa notices and smiles.

Susie addresses the girls.

>   SUSIE JENNINGS
>   Thank you all so much from coming
>   out to volunteer today. We will be
>   serving nearly ten thousand
>   homeless men and women and we want
>   them to feel as welcome and loved
>   as possible. This is our
>   opportunity to show them the love
>   of Jesus which they may have never
>   experienced before in their lives.
>   Your service will be the testimony
>   of His love for them.

The girls smile and nod in agreement.

>   SUSIE JENNINGS (CONT'D)
>   I believe each of you know the
>   areas you have been assigned to.
>   Depending on how long you can stay
>   you may want to volunteer in
>   multiple spots. Most of all, have
>   fun.

The girls pair off based on their assignments. Morgan steps over to Alyssa.

>   MORGAN
>   I think we're the foot washers.

>   ALYSSA
>   Hi, I'm Alyssa.

>   MORGAN
>   Morgan.

INT. DALLAS CONVENTION CENTER - LATER

Morgan and Alyssa kneel in front of two HOMELESS MEN who sit
in chairs. The girls wash the men's feet and put lotion on
them.

Alyssa slides new socks on the man's feet and hands him a new
pair of shoes.

                    ALYSSA
          There you go. New socks and shoes.
          You're all set.

                    HOMELESS MAN
          Thank you. I've never had my feet
          washed by someone before.

                    ALYSSA
          To be honest, until today I've
          never washed someone's feet before.

The man smiles and stands to leave.

Alyssa raises her hand and a VOLUNTEER guides another man,
GEORGE, to her station.

                    ALYSSA (CONT'D)
          Hi, I'm Alyssa, what's your name?

                    GEORGE
          George.

                    ALYSSA
          Nice to meet you George. You ready
          for some new shoes and socks.

                    GEORGE
          Yes, ma'am. I been wearing these so
          long I think they may have stuck to
          my feet.

                    ALYSSA
          Well, we'll take care of you.

Alyssa, begins to remove the dirty, crusty shoes and socks.
She tries to cover her reaction to the smell.

Morgan watches as she finishes with the man whose feet she is
cleaning.

                    MORGAN
          You're good as new, sir.

                    HOMELESS MAN 2
          Thank you, pretty lady.

                    MORGAN
          If you'll follow this man, he will
          take you to get a haircut if you
          want.

Morgan raises her hand and the Volunteer brings another man
to her station.

                    MORGAN (CONT'D)
               (to Alyssa)
          After this person, I could use a
          break.

                    ALYSSA
          Agreed. You think that will be
          okay?

                    MORGAN
          I'm sure.

A new man sits in front of Morgan.

                    MORGAN (CONT'D)
          Hi, how are you doing today?

INT. DALLAS CONVENTION CENTER - LATER

Morgan and Alyssa sit behind the curtains. Alyssa drinks
water and eats a power bar. Morgan sips from a water bottle.

                    ALYSSA
          All that scrubbing made me hungry.

Alyssa offers a power bar to Morgan, who declines.

                    MORGAN
          I had a big breakfast.

                    ALYSSA
          Who knew washing feet could be so
          difficult?

                    MORGAN
          OMG, did you see the corns on the
          one guy's feet? I swear they were
          as big as his toes.

                    ALYSSA
          Poor guy.

                    MORGAN
          I didn't know how to handle it.

                    ALYSSA
          Makes you appreciate what you have.

                    MORGAN
          Totally.

                    ALYSSA
          Have you ever volunteered for this
          before?

                    MORGAN
          No. But, I'm going to from now on.

The two each take a drink of water.

                    ALYSSA
          So, I noticed you sizing me up
          earlier. How do I compare to the
          others?

Morgan reacts to Alyssa's directness.

                    MORGAN
          Direct much?

                    ALYSSA
          Don't deny it.

                    MORGAN
          I won't.

                    ALYSSA
          So?

                    MORGAN
          How long have you been competing?

                    ALYSSA
          This is my first year. Well, I did
          some really small pageants like
          Miss Fall Festival and stuff like
          that. Nothing like this.

                    MORGAN
          Kind of different.

                    ALYSSA
          No kidding. Y'all take this stuff
          seriously.

                    MORGAN
          Well, sure. Not only does it
          provide scholarship for college but
          it can really springboard your
          career.

                    ALYSSA
          Legit.

                    MORGAN
          Callie, the girl handing out coats
          over there...

Morgan points to CALLIE PARKER, a beautiful young lady who is
handing out jackets.

                    MORGAN (CONT'D)
          She and I have been competing since
          we were in grade school. We were
          both Pageant Princesses - yes,
          that's a thing - then we both got
          involved with the Cinderella
          pageants.

                    ALYSSA
          I had no idea it was so involved.

                    MORGAN
          Oh yeah. There are feeder systems
          to prepare girls for our
          organization. And, we even have
          programs to train girls who think
          they may want to compete.

                    ALYSSA
          Like minor league teams?

                    MORGAN
          Kind of.

                    ALYSSA
          Sorry, my dad is a huge sports nut.

                    MORGAN
          Mine too. It's more of a sisterhood
          with littler sisters and big
          sisters.

                    ALYSSA
          So you're close to many of the
          girls?

                         MORGAN
               I love so many of them. We've been
               competing for so long it feels like
               a big sorority.

                         ALYSSA
               That's what I'm hoping for.

                         MORGAN
               You've come to the right place.

The girls smile are each other.

INT. ALVAREZ'S HOME OFFICE - DAY

Camilla and Ramon sit at a desk, a stack of bills, legal pad
and calculator in front of them.

                         CAMILLA
               But she's going to need these
               things if she's going to compete.
               That's just what it takes.

                         RAMON
               We might as well take the money to
               Choctaw and put it on the roulette
               wheel. The odds of return are about
               the same.

                         CAMILLA
               You're missing the point.

                         RAMON
               Apparently it's lost in all the
               expenses. What if she doesn't win?
               Then it's money --

Alyssa enters, shutting down the conversation.

                         CAMILLA
               Hi, honey? How was the appearance?

                         ALYSSA
               It was really fun. I got to know
               some of the girls. What are y'all
               doing?

                         CAMILLA
               Your father and I are just going
               over the family budget.

                         ALYSSA
               Is everything okay?

                         CAMILLA
              We'll manage, sweetie. Don't worry.
              Did you eat? Let me make you
              something.

Camilla exits.

Ramon, collects the papers and places them in a folder.

                         ALYSSA
              I know you don't want me to
              compete.

                         RAMON
              It's not that, monkey. It's just -
              Since your mom lost her job, things
              are really tight.

                         ALYSSA
              That's why I need the scholarship.

                         RAMON
              But the amount we are spending in
              the hopes you win, that could just
              go towards school.

                         ALYSSA
              I know dad, but I really want to do
              this and I'm learning there is so
              much more to it.

                         RAMON
              Like...?

                         ALYSSA
              Well, I'm still learning.

Ramon smiles.

                         RAMON
              Honey, you know I want to support
              your every dream.

                         ALYSSA
              I know.

                         RAMON
              But this one, right now, is really
              tough.

INT. MORGAN'S PARENT'S HOME - LIVING ROOM - DAY

Morgan models an incredible evening gown. Her mother and
Tommy inspect her.

                    TOMMY
          I think you look truly amazing!

Morgan smiles.

                    JOANNE
          But she wore it last year.

Morgan's smile disappears.

                    TOMMY
          That doesn't matter.

                    MORGAN
          Yeah, mom. Sydney literally wore
          her dress three years in a row and
          she won.

                    TOMMY
          Exactly. It's new judges every year
          so, it's not like anyone will
          remember.

                    JOANNE
          I will.

Morgan rolls her eyes.

                    JOANNE (CONT'D)
          Does it look like it is too tight?

Morgan smooths the fabric on her stomach.

                    TOMMY
          Not at all. (beat) Try on your
          talent costume.

                    JOANNE
          That needs to be updated too.

Morgan leaves the room exasperated with her mother.

INT. DRESS BOUTIQUE - DAY

Camilla and PAULA, Alyssa's local director - a woman so sweet
and accommodating but also as cunning as a fox - sit on a
sofa in front of a mini-runway.

Alyssa shyly steps out from behind the curtain of her
dressing room. She is uncomfortable being the center of
attention.

She awkwardly walks the small runway to show off the dress
she is wearing.

ARMANDO, stylish and gay, helps Alyssa with the train of the
dress.

                    ARMANDO
          Is this not the most stunning gown
          you have ever seen?

Alyssa smiles and twirls. Wrapping herself in the train which
Amarndo rushes to straighten.

                    ALYSSA
          Sorry.

                    ARMANDO
          This really isn't a twirl dress.

                    ALYSSA
          So, what do you think, mom?

                    CAMILLA
          It's gorgeous.

                    PAULA
          How do you feel in it?

                    ALYSSA
          Like Audrey Hepburn.

Alyssa twirls again. Armando, horrified, fixes the train
again.

                    ALYSSA (CONT'D)
          Sorry, Armando.

He fake smiles.

Paula takes a photo with her cell phone.

Camilla stands and not so subtly checks the price tag.

                    CAMILLA
          I would love to see you try on some
          others.

                    ARMANDO
          We'll try on the emerald one.

Armando helps Alyssa back into the dressing room.

> PAULA
> Do you mind me asking, what the
> budget is for a dress?

> CAMILLA
> You probably won't like the answer.

> PAULA
> I have taken girls to state in
> everything from a five thousand
> dollar dress to something they
> found at a department store.

> CAMILLA
> Really?

> PAULA
> Yes! It is not the price of the
> dress the judges are looking at.
> It's how the girl wears the dress.
> Or, does the dress wear the girl.

> CAMILLA
> So how do they judge?

> PAULA
> They're looking to see if the girl
> is confident. Does she command
> attention when she walks on stage.
> For the most part they are looking
> at the girl and her presence in the
> dress.

> CAMILLA
> So the design of the dress really
> doesn't matter?

> PAULA
> I didn't say that. I have seen some
> truly hideous dresses cross that
> stage and trust me, the judges are
> thinking, if the girl picked that
> dress we are not picking that girl.
> The dress and the girl have to say
> style and class.

Armando steps out of the dressing room.

> ARMANDO
> Get ready ladies, this dress may be
> even more stunning on her.

Alyssa steps out in a form fitting emerald mermaid style gown. It is figure flattering and compliments Alyssa perfectly.

She walks across the platform to stand and model in front of her mother and Paula. Paula snaps another phone photo.

> PAULA
> See how she simply flows across the stage? Effortlessly. This is what I'm talking about.

Alyssa is all smiles.

> ALYSSA
> Mom, I thought the other dress was perfect but this one is truly perfect? What do you think?

Alyssa twirls like a young girl, then catches herself.

> ARMANDO
> No, good ahead. This dress you can twirl in.

Alyssa completes the twirl.

> CAMILLA
> It is a beautiful gown. Are you comfortable?

Camilla motions to her chest.

Alyssa pulls the dress up in front.

> ALYSSA
> It's form fitting. But I like it.

Camilla, again, checks the price tag.

> CAMILLA
> Okay. Let's see the next one.

Alyssa frowns and walks back to the dressing room with Armando in tow.

INT. DRESS BOUTIQUE - DRESSING ROOM - SAME

Alyssa tries fitting into what is without a doubt a truly dreadful gown.

Morgan enters.

                    MORGAN
          Hey, stranger.

                    ALYSSA
          Hey.

Alyssa awkwardly struggles with her dress.

Morgan watches.

                    MORGAN
          No. Just no.

Armando peeks behind the curtain.

                    ARMANDO
          Oh dear God. How did that travesty
          even make it into the boutique?

                    MORGAN
          I just told her.

                    ARMANDO
          Thank you.

                    ALYSSA
          Yes, thank you. I would have died
          to be seen in this.

                    ARMANDO
          Let me see what I can do about he
          price of the emerald dress. (beat)
          Morgan, the gown your mom picked
          out is hanging here.

Armando points to a garment bag.

                    ARMANDO (CONT'D)
          We had it special ordered.

He steps outs.

Alyssa takes off her gown. She is self-conscious in front of
Morgan, hiding herself as much as possible. Morgan notices.

Morgan unzips the bag to reveal a gown that is perfect and
stunning in every way.

Alyssa hides her jealously by concentrating on putting on her
normal, street clothes.

Morgan changes into the dress. Nothing fazes this girl.

                    MORGAN
          Would you mind zipping me?

Alyssa zips up the gown and steps back to look at Morgan who
is the epitome of glamour.

                    ALYSSA
          That dress is amazing.

                    MORGAN
          It better be for what we're about
          to pay.

Alyssa looks at the emerald dress on the hanger. Morgan
follows her gaze.

                    MORGAN (CONT'D)
          Honestly, I would be just as happy
          wearing what I wore last year, but
          mom insists we have something new.

Alyssa smiles.

                    MORGAN (CONT'D)
          That's a beautiful dress. You going
          to get it?

                    ALYSSA
          I don't think so. It - It would
          need too much work... Ya know.

Alyssa looks at the dress longingly.

                    MORGAN
          I know the best seamstress who
          could do whatever needs to be done.

                    ALYSSA
          Yeah, but that would just add to --

                    MORGAN
          She pretty reasonable with her
          fees.

                    ALYSSA
          Thanks. I'll let you know.

Armando peaks his head in.

                    ARMANDO
          Everything okay in here? Oh my God!

                    MORGAN
          Yes. Coming out.

Alyssa picks up her purse.

                    MORGAN (CONT'D)
          Hey, you want to grab brunch?

                    ALYSSA
          Now?

                    MORGAN
          Yeah. I need a break from my mom.
          You would be doing me a huge favor.

                    ALYSSA
          Sure. I guess.

                    MORGAN
          Great. This won't take but a
          second. I know my mom. She'll buy
          this on the spot.

Morgan exits to the cheers of Joanne and Armando.

Alyssa, looks at the emerald dress once more then exits the
dressing room.

INT. RESTAURANT - DAY

Morgan and Alyssa sit in a hipster, aesthetically pleasing
restaurant having brunch. They laugh as they enjoy each
other's company.

                    MORGAN
          Beauty is pain. Especially on our
          bank accounts. That's what my dad
          says.

                    ALYSSA
          I think our dad's would really get
          along.

                    MORGAN
          We call him, Pageant Dad. He's been
          involved so long he knows more than
          the actual judges.

                    ALYSSA
          That's cool.

                    MORGAN
          How 'bout your dad?

                    ALYSSA
          He tries to be supportive.

                    MORGAN
          My dad wasn't always. He had to get
          to know the organization beyond
          just the pageantry.

                    ALYSSA
          What do you mean?

                    MORGAN
          Once he got to know the people
          involved he started to change his
          mind. That and when he thought it
          was all just gowns and swimsuits he
          missed the most important part.

                    ALYSSA
          The scholarships?

                    MORGAN
          Not even that. There are so many
          intangible benefits that so
          outweigh the whole money thing.

                    ALYSSA
          Like what?

                    MORGAN
          I've met TV personalities,
          athletes. I met the governor once.
          He told me if I ever wanted to go
          into politics he would back me. As
          if.

Morgan moves the food around on her plate but does not take a
bit.

                    ALYSSA
          We just met Susie Jennings last
          week.

                    MORGAN
          Exactly. Winning a title opens
          doors and gives you access to
          people you may never meet. Plus,
          the only reason I have the
          confidence I do, is because I've
          been talking in front of adults
          since I was like five.

                    ALYSSA
          Wish I had.

                    MORGAN
          Those are the intangibles. My dad
          totally gets it now.

                    ALYSSA
          You're mom seems pretty involved.

                    MORGAN
          She used to compete so, this is her
          whole world.

                    ALYSSA
          Where did she compete?

                    MORGAN
          New York. A million years ago, but
          to her it was like yesterday.

                    ALYSSA
          So, your mom got you into pageants?

                    MORGAN
          Yeah. I think she's living
          vicariously through me.

Alyssa notices that Morgan plays with her food more than she
eats it.

                    MORGAN (CONT'D)
          I love my mom, don't get me wrong.

                    ALYSSA
          Of course.

                    MORGAN
          It's just, sometimes I'm like,
          lighten up. Ya know?

                    ALYSSA
          Sure.

                    MORGAN
          It's one thing to compete and want
          to win, but it's another when
          winning is the only reason to
          compete. I love hanging out with
          the girls. And, my director has
          become like family.

                    ALYSSA
          Do your friends support you?

                    MORGAN
          Honestly, most of my friends are
          other pageant girls. They get it.

                    ALYSSA
          Yeah. It's like my friends say they
          support me, but then I feel like
          they mostly act jealous when I
          mention what I'm doing.

                    MORGAN
          It's passive aggressive behavior.

                    ALYSSA
          Totally! That's what it is.

                    MORGAN
          Ask anyone, we've all experienced
          it. That's why we stick together.

Morgan puts her fork down.

                    MORGAN (CONT'D)
          Would you excuse me a second?

                    ALYSSA
          Of course.

Morgan gets up and walks to the bathroom.

Alyssa checks her phone then sips her orange juice. Some of
it drops on her blouse. She tries to dab at it but only makes
it worse.

INT. RESTAURANT - BATHROOM - CONTINUOUS

Alyssa enters the bathroom and walks to the sink to wash her
blouse.

Sounds of GAGGING AND VOMITING come from the furthest stall.

Alyssa leaves the room quietly.

INT. RESTAURANT - LATER

Morgan returns to the table. Alyssa still tries to clean her
blouse with a napkin and water.

                    MORGAN
               What happened?

> ALYSSA
> A little spill. I'm so clumsy.

Morgan reaches into her purse and pulls out a Shout wipe.

> MORGAN
> Here. Use this. These are life
> savers.

Alyssa takes the cloth out and wipes the stain. It disappears almost immediately.

> ALYSSA
> Wow. Awesome. Thanks.

> MORGAN
> Glad to help.

Morgan drops cash into the bill folder without even looking at the cost.

> MORGAN (CONT'D)
> This is on me. Shall we go? I've
> got dance rehearsal.

INT. DANCE STUDIO - AFTERNOON

Morgan dances before a mirror. Her movements are exquisite, timed perfectly to the music. It is like she is another person when she dances, unencumbered from the worries of the world.

Suddenly a voice --

> JOANNE (O.C.)
> Point your toes!

More dancing. Graceful and pure.

> JOANNE (O.C.) (CONT'D)
> Arch your back more!

Morgan falls out of a pirouette early.

> JOANNE (CONT'D)
> No! It's supposed to be --

> MORGAN
> Mom! Stop!

> JOANNE
> It's almost perfect. I'm just
> trying to help.

                         MORGAN
                But you're not. Can you please wait
                in the hall?

Joanne exits the studio.

INT. ALVAREZ'S KITCHEN - AFTERNOON

Alyssa and Paula sit at the kitchen table. Alyssa has her
laptop open and is typing.

                         ALYSSA
                How does this sound?

Paula takes a moment to read the text.

                         PAULA
                Much better, but your platform
                statement should explain *your*
                emotional connection to the issue
                as much as why it is important for
                society.

                         ALYSSA
                My friend was misdiagnosed with
                depression instead of bipolar
                disorder and they prescribed the
                wrong medicine. It nearly killed
                her. I want people to know that
                with proper treatment, bipolar
                disorder can be taken care of.

                         PAULA
                Put that in your there.

Paula points to the computer.

                         ALYSSA
                What about all the statistics I
                have?

                         PAULA
                We can add some, but the judges
                care more about your connection.
                Girls used to randomly selected a
                platform like they were ordering
                off of a menu.

                         ALYSSA
                Okay.

Alyssa types more as Paula watches over her shoulder.

                    PAULA
          Make sure to mention how you would
          like to improve the situation.
          Don't be vague. The more action
          points you can make of how you will
          personally be involved the better.

                    ALYSSA
          With my friend's help, I've written
          a list of symptoms family members
          can look for.

                    PAULA
          Good. Mention that.

                    ALYSSA
          I also, want to publish a workbook
          for those dealing with the disorder
          and those that love them. They can
          work through it together.

                    PAULA
          That's a great idea. You can
          mention that as a step you wish to
          take if you become the state title
          holder.

                    ALYSSA
          Should I mention the foundation
          that I'm working with?

                    PAULA
          Absolutely. Lends credibility and
          shows you're already active for the
          cause.

Alyssa continues typing.

INT. MORGAN'S APARTMENT - NIGHT

Morgan sits in her college apartment surrounded by text
books. She talks on the phone.

                    MORGAN
          I made it fine, Mom. I've literally
          got a ton of material to catch on
          up for the classes I missed. (beat)
          I love you too. Sometimes, you just
          need to tone it down. You're not
          Kitty Carter. Tell dad, I love him.

Morgan disconnects and picks up one of her text books.

A KNOCK at her door.

Frustrated by another interruption Morgan drops her book and crosses the room to answer the door.

TROY HARPER, a typical college kid, enters, planting a kiss on Morgan the moment she opens the door.

> TROY
> I missed you so much.

> MORGAN
> I was only gone four days.

> TROY
> It seemed longer.

> MORGAN
> Maybe you should have driven to
> Dallas to watch me compete.

He carries Morgan across the room to the couch.

> TROY
> Ate a little too much of your mom's
> cooking, huh?

> MORGAN
> Don't be a jerk.

> TROY
> I would've come up, but my boys had
> a big thing planned this weekend. I
> couldn't bail on them.

> MORGAN
> You mean the kegger at the frat
> house?

> TROY
> You heard about it?

> MORGAN
> Dummy, you invited me and I told
> you I couldn't go.

> TROY
> Right.

Troy gets handsie with Morgan.

> TROY (CONT'D)
> But, you're here now.

                    MORGAN
          Studying.

Both are frustrated with the other.

                    TROY
          C'mon, I haven't seen you in like --

                    MORGAN
          Four days.

                    TROY
          Four long days. You look so hot.

He tries to kiss her again.

                    MORGAN
          Troy! You're just horny and I have
          to study.

                    TROY
          Ugh.

                    MORGAN
          That's what happens when you miss
          class.

                    TROY
          Listen, we're having a big event
          this weekend. You're coming, right?

                    MORGAN
          Can't.

                    TROY
          What? Why not? It's gonna be huge.

                    MORGAN
          Sorry. I have an appearance and my
          director set up mock interviews for
          me.

                    TROY
          Blow it off.

                    MORGAN
          I have responsibilities as a title
          holder.

                    TROY
          You have responsibilities to your
          boyfriend too.

He grabs her around the waist and draws her close for a kiss.
She returns his kiss, then stops before it can get out of
hand.

                    MORGAN
          You knew about this before we
          started dating. You said you were
          cool with it.

                    TROY
          I'm cool with having a beauty queen
          girlfriend, but what's the point if
          you're always too busy to go out?

                    MORGAN
          I hope you don't just go out with
          me because I won a pageant?

                    TROY
          Of course not.

Morgan pushes him away.

                    TROY (CONT'D)
          C'mon let's make up.

                    MORGAN
          And make out?

                    TROY
          Sounds good to me.

Troy moves closer. Morgan stands and walks away.

                    MORGAN
          I'll call you later.

Disappointed, Troy stands and leaves.

INT. ALYSSA'S APARTMENT - NIGHT

Alyssa enters her college apartment. Her roommates, KRISTI
and YASMINE, two young women caught between hipster and emo.
They sit on the sofa eating ice cream and watching reality
TV.

Kristi and Yasmine raise their spoons in salute and greeting
but don't bother to get up or shutoff the TV.

                    KRISTI
          Hey! There she is Miss... What's
          your title again?

                    ALYSSA
          Allen.

                    KRISTI
          That's it. Congrats.

                    ALYSSA
          Thanks.

                    YASMINE
          Very exciting stuff.

                    KRISTI
          Did you get like a crown and sash
          and stuff?

                    ALYSSA
          Yeah.

                    KRISTI
          Can I see?

                    ALYSSA
          I had to leave it at my parent's.

                    KRISTI
          Bummer.

                    YASMINE
          Yeah, we could have played dress
          up. Or worn it for Halloween.

                    ALYSSA
          Well, it's a little more important -

Yasmine nudges Kristi to get her to focus her attention on
the TV.

                    YASMINE
          Can you believe she is making out
          with that loser?

Kristi returns her attention to the reality show she and
Yasmine are watching.

                    KRISTI
          Ugh. I am shook.

Alyssa watches them, dumbfounded by their lack of real
excitement.

She walks toward her bedroom towing her small suitcase behind
her.

                              KRISTI (CONT'D)
                    We bought you a pint of ice cream.
                    It's Halo so you should be able to
                    eat it without feeling guilty.

                              ALYSSA
                    That's sweet. Thanks.

                              YASMINE
                    Come sit with us.

                              ALYSSA
                    Let me put my bag away.

Alyssa rolls her bag into her room then returns.

She curls up on the sofa with her friends. They are squashed
in a seat that normally should hold only two.

                              YASMINE
                    Are you as surprised as we are that
                    you won?

                              ALYSSA
                    A little I guess, but I went hoping
                    to win. Why? Are you surprised?

                              YASMINE
                    Well, no offense, but when I look
                    at you, I just don't think Miss
                    America.

                              ALYSSA
                    Wow. Thanks. You know, I'm kinda
                    tired.

Alyssa gets up and walks into her room, closing the door
behind her.

                              KRISTI
                    Uncool.

INT. ALYSSA'S APARTMENT - BEDROOM - CONTINUOUS

Alyssa sits on the edge of her bed, crestfallen. With friends
like her's, who needs enemies.

Her phone CHIMES. She received a text. The text is from
Morgan and it reads: CAN YOU TALK? FACETIME?

Alyssa, dials Morgan, whose face appears on Alyssa's phone
screen.

CROSS CUT BETWEEN ALYSSA AND MORGAN'S APARTMENTS

                    ALYSSA
        What's up, girl?

Tears stain Morgan's cheeks and he mascara is smudged. She
wipes her eyes and her mouth. Alyssa notices.

                    MORGAN
        Ugh. Boys!

                    ALYSSA
        The worst.

                    MORGAN
        Right?

                    ALYSSA
        Some girls aren't much better. What
        boy, specifically, are we talking
        about?

                    MORGAN
        My boyfriend, Troy.

                    ALYSSA
        Not the welcome home you were
        expecting?

                    MORGAN
        Thankfully I have very low
        expectations. He literally called
        me fat.

                    ALYSSA
        Seriously?

                    MORGAN
        Yes!

                    ALYSSA
        Girl, if I looked as good as you, I
        wouldn't be so scared to wear the
        bikini on stage.

                    MORGAN
        You're gorgeous.

                    ALYSSA
        I have night terrors about that
        part of competition.

                    MORGAN
        It's so easy.

                    ALYSSA
          For you. (beat) Tell me what Troy
          said.

                    MORGAN
          Literally, only wants to fool
          around or get drunk.

                    ALYSSA
          So, your typical frat boy?

                    MORGAN
          Exactly. He loved having a
          girlfriend in pageants. I think he
          tries to impress his friends. But --

                    ALYSSA
          The idea and the actuality aren't
          matching up.

                    MORGAN
          Yep.

                    ALYSSA
          I'm sorry.

                    MORGAN
          Thanks. I shouldn't let him upset
          me.

Morgan trails off and Alyssa waits for her to continue.
Finally to break the silence...

                    ALYSSA
          Morgan, you know you're beautiful,
          right?

                    MORGAN
          Sure.

                    ALYSSA
          No. Seriously.

                    MORGAN
          Tell that to my mother.

                    ALYSSA
          I thought she totally supported
          you?

                    MORGAN
          She does, but there's always room
          for improvement.

                    ALYSSA
          You realize you're making me want
          to drop out of competing?

Morgan laughs.

                    ALYSSA (CONT'D)
          If you have room for improvement,
          then my chances are about as good
          as Snoop Dog passing a drug test.

                    MORGAN
          That's a really weird analogy.

                    ALYSSA
          Yeah, I'm not good at those.

                    MORGAN
          You're really not. You should
          probably stop trying.

The two girls laugh.

                    ALYSSA
          No, but really, Morgan, you are
          stunning, talented and intelligent,
          and if your boyfriend, or mom,
          can't see that then they need to
          check again.

                    MORGAN
          Thanks, Aly. I appreciate that.

                    ALYSSA
          Don't let them taint your view of
          yourself, okay?

                    MORGAN
          I'm thankful for you.

                    ALYSSA
          You too, girl.

INT. OFFICE RECEPTION AREA - DAY

Morgan stands with Joanne and Tommy in the waiting area of a
small office.

                    TOMMY
          You know the drill.

                    MORGAN
     Yep.

                    TOMMY
          Ready?

INT. CONFERENCE ROOM - LATER

Morgan walks into the conference room and stands behind a
high-back chair in front of a table, facing THREE MOCK
JUDGES.

                    MOCK JUDGE 1
          Immigration is a hot topic, what
          with the recent Supreme Court
          decision to block travel for
          certain countries. How do you think
          we should handle the demand for
          those that want to move here with
          national security?

                    MORGAN
          There is no one simple solution.
          People are taking sides and not
          listening to each other and the
          truth is that there are many facets
          to this issue. It is not about
          whether we should allow people from
          other countries into ours, nor just
          about national security. The real
          questions we need ask are what are
          the ramifications of not allowing
          those people to enter? Or, to allow
          them to enter? How will it affect
          the colleges, where many of these
          immigrants want to attend? What
          does that mean for current American
          students when it comes to
          acceptance rates? How will not
          allowing these immigrants into the
          country affect employment rates,
          taxes, health care and insurance?
          Where will they live? And how does
          it affect housing and rent costs?
          This is a much bigger issue than
          either side is talking about
          because they have made it about
          race and religion.

                    MOCK JUDGE 2
          So what is your solution?

MORGAN
To be honest, I have not completely
studied all of the facts from
either side, so I do not have a
solution. If I did, maybe I should
run for president instead of Miss
Texas.

Everyone laughs.

MORGAN (CONT'D)
I can tell you that I do believe we
need to protect our borders and the
people who currently call America
home. That should be our number one
priority.

MOCK JUDGE 3
You have competed in this
organization for many years and not
won, why do you think this year you
should be crowned?

MORGAN
Good question. I have had a great
time competing in years past and
every year I learn and gain more
experience. I believe I am the girl
for the job because I fully
understand what the job requires
and what will be expected of me. As
you can tell, I am committed to
this organization and will give it
one hundred and fifty percent.

MOCK JUDGE 2
Your platform is Allergy Awareness.
What made you select this as your
platform?

MORGAN
My father is a doctor. I hope to
follow in his footsteps one day and
would love to open a practise with
him. While I do not personally
suffer from allergies, I have seen
first hand the difficulties it can
bring to someone's life if not
treated properly. From the simple
seasonal allergies, to more serious
nut and food allergies, it amazes
me that someone could die just from
touching a peanut.

                    MOCK JUDGE 2
          I deal with that.

                    MORGAN
          So you know how serious allergies
          can be. My platform is about
          bringing awareness of the issue and
          having early detection as well as
          trying to find a cure if there is
          one. We talk about curing so many
          diseases, can we find a cure for
          allergies? I would like to try.

Tommy pops his head into the room.

                    TOMMY
          Time. Morgan if you will step out
          in the hallway.

Morgan faces the Mock Judges.

                    MORGAN
          Thank you.

INT. SOUNDS STUDIO - DAY

Alyssa stands with WT GREER, her vocal coach who is as silky
voiced and smooth talking as Frank Sinatra, if Frank were a
six foot two, black man.

WT has Alyssa warming up with vocal exercises.

                    WT GREER
          Fine. Fine. Let's get started.

Alyssa prepares her sheet music in front of her. WT sits down
at a piano and glances Alyssa's way to see if she is ready.

Alyssa nods and WT begins to play. Alyssa sings.

Between WT's playing and Alyssa's singing, angels stop their
heavenly duties to listen.

The song ends much too soon.

                    WT GREER (CONT'D)
          That was delicious. Simply
          delicious. If you don't win talent,
          I will personally come down there
          and get in those judges faces.

                    ALYSSA
          Let's hope it doesn't come to that.

                    WT GREER
          You know I'll do it too.

Alyssa smiles meekly.

                    ALYSSA
          Did the bridge sound okay? I felt
          like I was struggling.

WT plays the bridge and sings the part effortlessly.

                    ALYSSA (CONT'D)
          See. When you do it, it sounds
          flawless.

                    WT GREER
          Flattery will get you everywhere.
          Now you. Are you using your head or
          chest voice?

Alyssa sings the notes.

                    WT GREER (CONT'D)
          Head voice. Stay in your chest. You
          won't have to reach so far for the
          note.

                    ALYSSA
          Perfect.

WT stands and walks around the piano.

                    WT GREER
          You sound wonderful. You really do.
          I hate to bring this up, but...
          This is our fourth session and I
          would like to get caught up --

                    ALYSSA
          I'm sorry. I thought we had paid.

                    WT GREER
          Now, honey, I don't want you to
          stress this. It's really not a big
          deal. You know I've got you. But --

                    ALYSSA
          Of course. I'll talk with my
          parents.

                    WT GREER
          That's all I ask. Okay, now that
          that ugliness is out of the way,
          let me hear you sing "Just Keep
          Moving the Line."

Alyssa groans.

                    WT GREER (CONT'D)
          Excuse me?

                    ALYSSA
          That song is a killer.

                    WT GREER
          And so are you. You need to be that
          killer if you're going to take the
          stage. Nobody wants to watch a
          wallflower wail. Channel your inner
          diva.

WT pokes Alyssa in the stomach.

                    WT GREER (CONT'D)
          I know she's in there. Come out
          little diva!

EXT. COLLEGE AUDITORIUM - DAY

The Special Olympics are holding one of their annual events.
Children and adults with intellectual disabilities enter the
auditorium or are walking with supervisors to various events.

Morgan parks her car and walks across the street to enter the
auditorium.

INT. COLLEGE AUDITORIUM - CONTINUOUS

Morgan enters to find Alyssa and Callie sitting behind a long
table, their headshot photos and Sharpie pens at the ready to
provide signatures for those that ask.

                    ALYSSA
          Hey! I was hoping you were going to
          make it.

                    MORGAN
          Never miss it. What's this, our
          fifth year, Callie?

                    CALLIE
          Something like that.

While not entirely self-absorbed, Callie, is nearly robotic in her pageant perfect responses to those she needs to impress.

                    ALYSSA
          Callie and I were just getting to
          know each other.

                    MORGAN
          I was hoping you two would meet.
          So what's the plan? Same as before?

                    CALLIE
          Meet and greet, then participate in
          some of the less strenuous
          activities. Lot's of photo opps.

JIM, a coordinator between the pageant and the Special Olympics approaches. He is friendly and outgoing.

                    JIM
          Hi, Morgan. I'm glad you made it.

                    MORGAN
          Hi. Jim. I wouldn't miss it.

                    JIM
          We love having you all here. (beat)
          Callie, I would like to take you
          for a photo op with one of our
          sponsors. I'll come back for you
          girls once we're finished.

          MORGAN   ALYSSA
Great.   Great.

Morgan sits down next to Alyssa.

Callie leaves with Jim.

                    ALYSSA (CONT'D)
          She's really nice.

                    MORGAN
          I love her. She's become a bit of
          Pageant Patty though.

                    ALYSSA
          What's that?

                    MORGAN
          She's been doing this so long that
          everything is pre-programmed.
                    (MORE)

                    MORGAN (CONT'D)
You can tell she really doesn't
have the heart for it any longer.
It's the first runner up curse.

                    ALYSSA
What's that?

                    MORGAN
It get's in a girl's head. She
thinks, 'I almost won, so the next
year I will.' They put so much
pressure on themselves, they
crater. Happened to Callie.

                    ALYSSA
Really?

                    MORGAN
Don't say anything.

                    ALYSSA
What happened?

                    MORGAN
She went from first runner up to
not even making the top five.
Crushed her, but she knew it was
her own fault. She's back better
than ever now.

A YOUNG MAN comes up to the table.

                    YOUNG MAN
May I have a photo?

                    ALYSSA
Of course! Would you like me to
sign it to you.

                    YOUNG MAN
Yes, please.

Alyssa signs her photo and hands it to the Young Man.

                    ALYSSA
Morgan has her photo as well. Would
you like one?

                    YOUNG MAN
Yes, please.

Morgan's photos are pre-signed and she hands it to the man.

                    MORGAN
          How about a photo together?

                    YOUNG MAN
          That would be great.

                    MORGAN
          Let's do it then.

Morgan and Alyssa stand behind the Young Man as he positions
his camera with arm extended to take the photo of the three
of them.

                    YOUNG MAN
          Thank you.

                    MORGAN
          Thank you.

                    ALYSSA
          Have fun today.

The Young Man walks away.

                    ALYSSA (CONT'D)
          So any news with Troy?

                    MORGAN
          He's still mad that I didn't cancel
          coming here.

                    ALYSSA
          Not very understanding.

                    MORGAN
          Literally the least understanding
          person ever. What about you? Any
          boy troubles?

                    ALYSSA
          My trouble is not having a boy.

                    MORGAN
          Trust me, you're better off. Prince
          Charming is not so charming once
          you get to know him.

Another intellectually disabled YOUNG MAN 2 arrives at the
table with his MOTHER.

                    MOTHER
          May he have a photo?

                    MORGAN
          Of course.

                    ALYSSA
          Would you like a photo of us
          together?

Young Man 2 reacts by withdrawing into his mother's side and
hiding his face.

                    MOTHER
          No, that's okay. He wanted to say
          hello but sometimes he gets shy
          meeting new people.

                    MORGAN
          We understand. I hope you have a
          great time today.

Young Man 2 and his Mother walk away.

Morgan smiles as they walk away.

                    MORGAN (CONT'D)
          What made you get into pageants?

                    ALYSSA
          It was really about the
          scholarships. Things have tight for
          my family for about a year now.

                    MORGAN
          I'm sorry.

                    ALYSSA
          I knew this was a long shot, but I
          thought, well, how hard can it be?
          Turns out, a lot harder than I
          thought, and on top of it I have
          ringers like you and Callie to
          compete with.

Morgan laughs.

                    MORGAN
          Thanks but, we're no ringers.
          Honestly, the biggest competition
          you have is yourself.

                    ALYSSA
          What do you mean?

                    MORGAN
          Literally, your mind is your
          competition. I have to fight
          negative thoughts about myself all
          the time.

                    ALYSSA
          Really?

                    MORGAN
          Totally.

Callie and Jim return.

                    JIM
          Okay, who wants to go next?

                    MORGAN
          Alyssa should go. I want to catch
          up with my girl.

EXT. COLLEGE AUDITORIUM - DAY

Jim leads Alyssa outside where a truck plastered with Dallas
Cowboys signage is parked. There is an interactive display of
team memorabilia.

Standing nearby are owner, JERRY JONES, and his daughter,
CHARLOTTE ANDERSON JONES.

                    JIM
          Alyssa, I'd like you to meets,
          Jerry and Charlotte Jones.

                    ALYSSA
          I'm so pleased to meet you. My dad
          is going to freak when I tell him I
          about this.

                    JERRY
          We're equally pleased to meet you.
          To bad your dad isn't here.

                    CHARLOTTE
          Congratulations on winning your
          title.

                    ALYSSA
          Thank you.

                    JIM
          Alyssa is one of our new
          contestants. This will be her first
          year competing on a state level.

                    CHARLOTTE
          That's exciting.

                    ALYSSA
          Oh my gosh.

                    JERRY
          You know, I've had a little
          experience being involved in
          competition for big prizes. (beat)
          My best advice is to enjoy the
          moment and leave everything you can
          on the field. Or, in your case, the
          stage.

                    ALYSSA
          Thank you. That's good advice.

                    JIM
          Shall we get a picture?

                    JERRY
          Absolutely!

                    ALYSSA
          My dad is going to be so jealous.

                    JERRY
          A fan I take it?

                    ALYSSA
          One of your biggest. We make him
          watch the games alone, he get's so
          stressed.

                    JERRY
          I know that feeling sometimes.

                    CHARLOTTE
          Trust me, we have that same
          problem.

They all laugh.

Alyssa stands between Charlotte and Jerry. Jim takes the
picture.

                    ALYSSA
          It was so nice meeting you both.

                    CHARLOTTE
          The pleasure was ours.

                    JERRY
          Tell your dad, we plan to keep his
          stress level down this year.

                    ALYSSA
          I will.

                    CHARLOTTE
          Good luck with the competition.

                    ALYSSA
          Thank you.

Alyssa and Jim walk away.

                    ALYSSA (CONT'D)
          I can't believe I just met Jerry
          Jones and Charlotte.

                    JIM
          The NFL are partners of the Special
          Olympics.

INT. COLLEGE AUDITORIUM - LATER

Large neon plastic drums have been placed to form a ring.
Alyssa, Morgan, Callie, have been joined by Tara, MADDIE and
SKYLER, other title holders. They each stand next to an
intellectually disabled person as they play the drum to the
beat of the music.

Everyone dances, laughs and has a good time.

The song ends. The HOST on stage takes the microphone and
speaks to the audience.

                    HOST
          All right! That was incredible. Are
          we all having fun?

The crowd cheers.

                    HOST (CONT'D)
          Great. Now we're going to open the
          stage to anyone who wants to sing
          some karaoke. Do we have any
          volunteers?

Alyssa, Morgan, Tara, Skyler and Maddie gather the Special
Olympic participants in front of the stage to listen.

                    MORGAN
               (to Alyssa)
          Let's hear what you got, girl.

                    ALYSSA
          No. That's okay.

                    MORGAN
          C'mon. You're going to be singing
          in front of a lot more people than
          this soon. Better get used to it.

Alyssa looks around the room. The look on her face betrays
her emotions.

                    ALYSSA
          I'm good. Let's let some of the
          kids have a turn.

INT. RESURANT - AFTERNOON

Alyssa, Morgan, Callie, Skyler and Maddie, sit in a booth
scarfing down burgers, fries and malts.

                    SKYLER
          I cannot believe we're doing this!

                    CALLIE
          Relax, we're allowed a cheat day
          every now and then.

                    MADDIE
          OMG. I forgot how good all of this
          is.

                    SKYLER
          I miss comfort food.

                    MORGAN
          I miss food.

The girls laugh.

                    CALLIE
          You will never convince me that
          rice cakes are real food.

                    SKYLER
          Right?

The table falls silent as the girls focus on devouring their
food. It is like a scene from a National Geographic episode
of lionesses eating a gazelle.

                    SKYLER (CONT'D)
          I may never be able to go back to
          quinoa and kale again.

The only response is low GRUNTS of agreement.

                    MADDIE
          How long do you think it will take
          to work this off?

                    CALLIE
          I'm shook.

                    SKYLER
          Can we not. I want to enjoy my
          fatty food.

                    MADDIE
          Easy for you, you don't have to
          worry about thigh gap and getting
          into a dance costume.

                    MORGAN
          Dancers never have thigh gap.

                    CALLIE
          So how do you do it?

                    MORGAN
          Just lucky, I guess.

Alyssa wipes her mouth. She notices that Morgan is not
eating.

                    ALYSSA
          You've got to be as hungry as the
          rest of us?

                    MORGAN
          I ate a power bar as I drove over.

                    SKYLER
          That's another food group I can do
          without ever eating again.

                    ALYSSA
          You ate something on the way to
          come eat?

                    MORGAN
          Don't make a thing out of it.

A tense air falls over the table.

Maddie chirps in to break the silence.

                    MADDIE
          Did you hear, Landon won Houston?

                    CALLIE
          Yes. She's going to be tough this
          year you guys. Those are great
          directors.

                    MADDIE
               (to Morgan)
          You were her roommate last year,
          right?

Morgan nods.

                    MORGAN
          She's the best. I love her.

                    ALYSSA
          What's her talent?

                    CALLIE
          She's a baton twirler.

                    SKYLER
          A good one.

                    CALLIE
          Jealous much?

                    SKYLER
          Just saying. I can admit I wish I
          was as good as her.

                    ALYSSA
          How does the roommate thing work?
          Do we get to pick?

                    MORGAN
          They're assigned.

                    MADDIE
          Usually, by group.

                    ALYSSA
          Group?

                    MORGAN
          Because there are so many girls
          competing, they separate us into
          smaller groups and we each perform
          different parts of the competition
          during prelims.

                    CALLIE
          You'll probably get assigned a girl
          in your group cause it makes things
          easier as you're prepping if you
          both have to be at the same place
          at the same time.

                    MADDIE
          It's like an extended sleep-over.

                    SKYLER
          We take over an entire floor of the
          hotel. It's awesome!

Morgan stands.

                    MORGAN
          I'm going to the bathroom.

Alyssa looks up at Morgan.

                    ALYSSA
          I'm come with.

                    MORGAN
          No. That's okay. Finish your fries.

                    ALYSSA
          I'm stuffed.

                    MORGAN
          I've been peeing on my own for
          years now.

                    ALYSSA
          I know, but I have to pee too.

Morgan stares at Alyssa, who isn't backing down. She stands.

Callie, Maddie and Skyler watch the stand-off. Confused.

                    MORGAN
          Go ahead then. I can hold it. I
          think it's a single stall anyway.

                    SKYLER
          No, there's two. I went earlier.

Morgan smiles an insincere smile.

>   CALLIE
>   You have a shy bladder or
>   something, Morgan?

>   MADDIE
>   How do you manage at state when we
>   share a bathroom?

>   SKYLER
>   Poo-pourii spray. It's a life
>   saver. Trust me.

Morgan grabs her purse.

>   MORGAN
>   I've got to go anyway. I can hold
>   it until I get home. See ya all.

Morgan leaves abruptly.

Callie, Skyler and Maddie sit wondering what just happened.
Alyssa watches as Morgan gets in her car and drives away.

INT. ALYSSA'S APARTMENT - BEDROOM - NIGHT

Alyssa sits on her bed and texts. She writes: HEY, GIRL. JUST
CHECKING IN. TODAY WAS FUN.

She sends the text.

INT. MORGAN'S APARTMENT - SAME

Morgan's phone CHIMES. She received a text. She checks her
phone and sees that it is from Alyssa. She ignores it and
puts her phone down.

INT. ALYSSA'S APARTMENT - BEDROOM - SAME

Alyssa sees that her text to Morgan was read and she waits
for a response, but none comes. She gets the old "read and
ignore."

INT. ALYSSA'S APARTMENT - LIVING ROOM

Yasmine and Kristi study on the sofa. Kristi looks up as
Alyssa comes out of her room.

                    KRISTI
          Come hang out with us.

Alyssa sits on a chair across from them.

                    ALYSSA
          What you studying?

                    KRISTI
          French.

                    YASMINE
          Statistics.

Yasmine nods her head like she has fallen asleep and SNORES.
She opens her eyes and laughs with the others.

                    ALYSSA
          You lead exciting lives.

                    YASMINE
          Well, we can't all be beauty
          queens.

Alyssa ignores her.

                    ALYSSA
          You want to get coffee, or
          something?

Kristi slams her book shut.

                    KRISTI
          Oui!

                    YASMINE
          If I don't figure this crap out I'm
          in trouble.

                    KRISTI
          From who, the math police?

                    ALYSSA
          Yeah, c'mon. We haven't hung out in
          forever.

                    YASMINE
          Whose fault is that?

                    ALYSSA
          We've all been busy.

                         YASMINE
              And now I have something to do. We
              don't all live by your schedule
              cause your a queen.

                         ALYSSA
              I wasn't saying th --

                         KRISTI
              Come on, Yas. Let's hang.

                         YASMINE
              You two go ahead.

Kristi jumps up from the sofa.

                         KRISTI
              Let me change my shirt.

Kristi exits into her room.

                         ALYSSA
              Look, I'm sorry if I did something
              to make you mad.

                         YASMINE
              You didn't. I just don't get this
              whole beauty queen thing.

                         ALYSSA
              You know why I felt I had to.

                         YASMINE
              Yeah, and I hope that works out for
              you. I do. I just miss my friend.

                         ALYSSA
              Then come out with us.
              Statistically speaking your odds
              may improve with caffeine in your
              system.

Yasmine smiles.

INT. MORGAN'S PARENT'S HOME - LIVING ROOM - DAY

Joanne and Tommy enter. They each carry numerous bags from
name brand clothing stores.

Anthony sits on the sofa watching college football when the
two enter and interrupt his relaxing Saturday.

                    JOANNE
          Wait 'till you see the bargins we
          got.

                    TOMMY
          You're wife really does know how to
          find the best deals.

                    ANTHONY
          It's the only reason we still have
          a roof over our head.

Joanne gives her husband a, don't be an ass, look.

                    TOMMY
          Yes, well, your daughter will be
          raising the roof with the new
          clothes we got her for appearances
          and interview.

                    ANTHONY
          Shouldn't Morgan have been with you
          to help select the clothes? Or, at
          least try them on?

                    JOANNE
          Oh, they'll fit, even if she needs
          to lose a few pounds.

Tommy steps back, not wanting to get caught in the cross-
fire.

                    JOANNE (CONT'D)
          Relax, honey. I've been doing this
          long enough to know what she needs.

Joanne takes the bags out of the room. Tommy stands awkwardly
with Anthony. He feigns interest in the football game on TV.

                    TOMMY
          So who's playing?

                    ANTHONY
          Tommy, you know I support what you
          do, but I want to make sure the
          primary focus is on Morgan, not on
          how much money you and my wife can
          spend.

                    TOMMY
          I know --

ANTHONY
You know better than most that it's
not about having the best clothes.

TOMMY
You're right. I'm sorry. It's just
so easy to go crazy, shopping with
Joanne. Have you ever tried to tell
your wife no? That's not so easy.

ANTHONY
I grant you that. Just do me a
favor.

TOMMY
Name it.

ANTHONY
Next time Joanne wants to go
shopping, have other plans.

INT. ALVAREZ HOME - KITCHEN - DAY

Alyssa, Camilla, Ramon, and Paula, sit around the kitchen
table covered with pageant paperwork. Paula tries to keep it
organized.

PAULA
All right, I think that does it.
Pretty painless.

RAMON
Until the check needs to be
written.

Camilla puts her hand on Ramon's arm and gives him a look as
if to say, "we discussed this."

PAULA
Yes, but we still have plenty of
time before any fees are due.

CAMILLA
It won't be a problem.

Ramon, HUFFS.

ALYSSA
Mom, Dad, if we can't afford it
then I don't need to compete.

Paula stops putting paper clips on pages and looks up
surprised.

                    PAULA
          I'll need to know if you cannot
          fulfill your obligation.

                    CAMILLA
          She will.

                    PAULA
          I'll would need to reach out to the
          runner ups to see if they want to
          take your place. Some have already
          received other local titles.

                    CAMILLA
          That won't be necessary.

Paula is genuinely concerned for Alyssa and her family.

                    PAULA
          I really love working with your
          daughter. I think she has a strong
          chance at state.

                    ALYSSA
          Do you really?

                    PAULA
          Absolutely. Your talent is amazing.
          You have a fantastic personality.

                    RAMON
          She gets that from me.

                    PAULA
          Obviously. There's no doubt in my
          mind, you're the type of girl
          they're looking for. But, I don't
          make any promises.

                    ALYSSA
          Of course.

                    PAULA
          It's truly in the judge's hands.

                    RAMON
          So you're saying there's no
          influence put on the judges?

                    PAULA
          Not that I'm aware of. In fact, the
          state directors rarely even
          interact with the judges once
          competition begins, to avoid even
          the appearance of collusion.

Paula places the paperwork in her bag.

                    RAMON
          Paula, let me ask you something.

                    PAULA
          Sure.

                    RAMON
          Does it makes sense to spend so
          much money in the hopes of getting
          just a portion of it back in
          scholarship?

                    PAULA
          I can't answer that for you, Ramon.
          I know the situation with Camilla's
          work, but the fact is this has to
          be your decision regardless of the
          outcome.

                    ALYSSA
          Dad, there's so much more than just
          the scholarship.

                    RAMON
          You say that but you haven't told
          me what that is.

                    ALYSSA
          I just met Jerry Jones. That would
          never have happened.

                    PAULA
          That's true. Lots of doors will
          open for your daughter.

                    CAMILLA
          Think of the opportunities that may
          open for here by being the state
          title holder.

                    RAMON
          I'm seriously outnumbered her.

The group laugh.

                    RAMON (CONT'D)
          You know I want to do everything
          for you.

                    ALYSSA
          I know, daddy.

Ramon grabs his heart.

                    RAMON
          Oh, the daddy card. That's playing
          dirty. Okay, I have some friends
          who own companies, if you -- and
          this will be solely your
          responsibility -- if you can get
          them to sponsor you to help offset
          some costs, then we can make this
          work.

                    PAULA
          That's a great idea, Ramon. Many
          girls do that. I can put together a
          presentation packet of benefits for
          the sponsors based on the level of
          commitment they will make.

                    RAMON
          I like that.

                    PAULA
          Alyssa, why don't you and I grab a
          coffee and discuss this some more.

INT. COFFEE SHOP - EARLY EVENING

Alyssa and Paula sit at a table in the corner of a hipster
coffee shop.

                    PAULA
          Your father is right. Raising money
          to pay for expenses is your
          responsibility.

                    ALYSSA
          I know. With classes and rehearsal,
          finding the time is going to be the
          real challenge.

                    PAULA
          You're going to have to make it
          happen. You have to make the
          effort.

                    ALYSSA
          I will.

                    PAULA
          I'll also see who I know that we
          can reach out to for nail and hair
          sponsorship.

                    ALYSSA
          That would be great.

                    PAULA
          But listen, nothing is free. You
          have to give them shout-outs on
          social media, head shots and be
          available for appearances at their
          business. There has to be some
          benefit for them other than getting
          to be in your presence.

Alyssa laughs.

Alyssa checks her text message thread with Morgan. There are
outgoing messages but Morgan has never responded.

                    PAULA (CONT'D)
          I talked to WT.

                    ALYSSA
          Yeah?

                    PAULA
          I'm going to cover what is owned.

                    ALYSSA
          No, I couldn't ask --

                    PAULA
          You didn't ask, I offered. It's
          done. I'm doing it. That will get
          you square and you can keep seeing
          him.

                    ALYSSA
          I really appreciate everything.

                    PAULA
          You know you're like family.

                    ALYSSA
          I feel the same.

                    PAULA
I want you to do well. I believe
you will but you can't have stress
weighing on you.

                    ALYSSA
I know.

                    PAULA
If you think it's stressful now
waiting until the week of
competition.

                    ALYSSA
I'll be ready.

                    PAULA
How's everything else going?

                    ALYSSA
Okay. I guess.

                    PAULA
That was the most unconvincing
answer I've ever heard in my life.

                    ALYSSA
No. It's fine. There's just a lot
going on.

                    PAULA
You have a good support group of
friends?

                    ALYSSA
They don't always understand why I
do this.

                    PAULA
Pageants have a stigma we're still
trying to overcome. For years we
were the "world peace" people. I
think you're learning it's so much
more.

                    ALYSSA
Exactly.

                    PAULA
Others will try to tear you down
but they don't have any power over
you unless you give it to them.

>   ALYSSA
> Yeah.

>   PAULA
> You know you can tell me anything?

>   ALYSSA
> Of course.

EXT. MORGAN'S PARENT'S HOME - BACKYARD - NIGHT

Sitting on a porch swing Morgan and Anthony take in the view of the sunset over the golf course which is their back yard.

>   ANTHONY
> Is everything okay, sweetie?

>   MORGAN
> Yeah. Of course, Dad.

>   ANTHONY
> Can I see your fingers?

Morgan goes on the defense.

>   MORGAN
> Why?

>   ANTHONY
> I just want to check something.

>   MORGAN
> Dad! I'm fine. Trust me. I haven't
> done that in a long time.

>   ANTHONY
> How long?

>   MORGAN
> Since... you know. I promise I'm
> better.

>   ANTHONY
> I'm just worried about you, kiddo.
> I know how much pressure you're
> under.

>   MORGAN
> You mean, how much pressure mom
> puts me under.

>   ANTHONY
> She means well.

                    MORGAN
          Her expectations are just
          unrealistic.

                    ANTHONY
          Hey, I know. I lived with her for
          five years before you came along.

The two laugh.

                    ANTHONY (CONT'D)
          You know, if it weren't for you,
          your mom might still be competing
          in the Mrs. system.

                    MORGAN
          Sometimes I think she resents me
          for that.

                    ANTHONY
          Not at all.

Morgan gives her dad a "come on" look.

                    ANTHONY (CONT'D)
          Seriously, she couldn't be happier.

                    MORGAN
          She can if I win.

                    ANTHONY
          Well, yeah. There's that.

                    MORGAN
          Why is winning so important to her?

                    ANTHONY
          I think because it's something she
          was never able to achieve and she
          wants it for you.

                    MORGAN
          It's honestly not that big of a
          deal to me.

                    ANTHONY
          Don't tell your mom that.

                    MORGAN
          Don't worry. I know better.

                    ANTHONY
          That's good for both of our sakes.

                    MORGAN
          But seriously. I enjoy competing
          and I love the girls, but if I
          never win, I honestly, won't be
          heartbroken.

                    ANTHONY
          Why do it then?

                    MORGAN
          I guess, for mom. Sometimes I
          literally feel like more of a
          project than a daughter.

Morgan's phone CHIMES. A text has arrived.

She checks to see a message from Alyssa. She ignores it.

                    ANTHONY
          Don't let me stop you from your
          life.

                    MORGAN
          No, it's okay.

                    ANTHONY
          Have you considered talking to your
          mother about how you feel?

                    MORGAN
          I get about five words out and she
          goes off on one of her monologues.

                    ANTHONY
          She is better at talking than
          listening.

                    MORGAN
          It's okay. I age out after this
          year. I've got one more competition
          in me.

EXT. COLLEGE CAMPUS - NIGHT

Alyssa walks across the quad. She holds her phone. She checks
to see if Morgan responded to her text.

Kristi and Yasmine run up behind her. They are extremely
happy and balance seems to be an issue. It appears they have
been drinking.

                    KRISTI
          Girl! Where've you been? We've been
          raging?

                    ALYSSA
          Looks like it.

                    YASMINE
          You totally missed out. We could go
          back. (to Kristi) You want to go
          back?

                    KRISTI
          Totes. Let's go.

They turn around and try to pull Alyssa with them.

                    ALYSSA
          No. Guys. I can't.

                    YASMINE
          Party pooper.

                    ALYSSA
          I just have some pageant stuff to
          take care of.

                    YASMINE
             (sarcastically)
          Yea! Pageant stuff.

                    KRISTI
          C'mon. You can take one night off
          to party with your girls.

                    YASMINE
          No, that wouldn't be deemed
          appropriate Kristi. Miss don't
          consort with the likes of us.

                    ALYSSA
          I never said anything like that.

                    YASMINE
          You didn't need to say it. We feel
          it.

                    ALYSSA
          What do you mean?

                    YASMINE
          Girl, ever since you won you've had
          this air about you.

                    ALYSSA
          I don't think I have --

                    YASMINE
          You may not think it, but you stink
          it.

Yasmine laughs at her own poor attempt at a joke.

                    ALYSSA
          I don't think you guys need any
          more to drink.

                    YASMINE
          See there you go, judging us.

                    ALYSSA
          I'm not judging you. I --

                    YASMINE
          Miss High and Mighty. Maybe that
          should be your title. Miss Better
          than everyone else.

                    ALYSSA
          I don't feel that way.

                    YASMINE
          Do you really think you're pretty
          enough to win? I mean, seriously?

Alyssa is uncomfortable and now even Kristi is realizing the
conversation is taking a dark turn.

                    KRISTI
          C'mon Yas, let's go get another
          drink.

                    YASMINE
          No. Hold on. I want to know the
          truth.

Yasmine points at Alyssa.

                    YASMINE (CONT'D)
          Be honest, do you really think you
          could be Miss America? I mean,
          kudos if you do.

Alyssa stands dumbstruck at her "friend's" behavior.

                    KRISTI
          C'mon, I'm thirsty.

                    YASMINE
          You know what's worse? You call
          yourself a feminist and yet your
          going to parade around on stage in
          a bikini and let others judge you.

                    ALYSSA
          You're right, that part of the
          competition does seem a bit dated,
          but the truth is a woman has
          nothing to feel ashamed about her
          body. And, a well rounded woman can
          be fit, talented and intelligent,
          which is exactly what the
          competition proves.

Yasmine is speechless for the first time.

                    ALYSSA (CONT'D)
          I bet you didn't know that many
          past contestants have gone on to be
          doctors, lawyers, journalists,
          politicians, and of course actors
          and singers. If pageants are good
          enough for Oprah Winfrey, Sarah
          Palin, Diane Sawyer and hundreds of
          others, then it's good enough for
          me.

Alyssa turns and walks away. Her friends stand awestruck by
her response. What they don't see are the tears in Alyssa's
eyes.

INT. ALYSSA'S COLLEGE BEDROOM - LATER

Alone in her apartment, Alyssa let's herself release the
flood of tears she has been holding.

She takes her phone out and looks at the many text messages
she has sent to Morgan with no response.

She dials Morgan's number.

INT. MORGAN'S PARENT'S BACKYARD - SAME

Morgan's phone rings. She sees Alyssa's name on CALLER ID and
ignores the call.

INT. ALYSSA'S COLLEGE BEDROOM - SAME

The call goes to VOICE MAIL. Alyssa, chokes back tears to
leave a message.

> ALYSSA
> Hi, Morgan. I could really use a
> friend. I'm sorry for whatever I
> did to upset you. I need to talk to
> someone who understands what I'm
> going through. I'm really stressed
> right now. I don't know. Maybe I
> should just drop out. Who am I
> trying to kid anyway?

There is only silence.

> ALYSSA (CONT'D)
> Well, call me.

Alyssa hangs up and begins to cry again.

She stops long enough to look in the mirror. She studies her
face.

Nearby sits a program book for pageant. The cover has a
photograph of the last winner. Alyssa holds the photo up next
to her face and looks in the mirror - comparing herself.

She tosses the book in disgust. If self esteem was a cookie,
Alyssa's would be nothing but crumbs.

INT. MORGAN'S APARTMENT - LATER

Morgan picks up her phone and listens to Alyssa's message.
She debates about whether to return the call, then decides
against it.

INT. HOTEL - BALLROOM - DAY

A large ballroom has been lined with chairs which are filled
with contestants and their parents. Morgan and Joanne sit on
one side of the room while Alyssa and Camilla sit on another
and behind them a few rows.

Morgan looks gaunt. She glances back over her shoulder to
Alyssa, who notices and smiles.

At the front of the room, standing behind a podium is PAMELA
WELLS, the state director and a woman whose personality is as
large as the state of Texas which she represents.

                    PAMELA
          Helloooo everyone. So glad y'all
          could make it to our spring
          meeting. We have so much
          information and fun stuff for y'all
          this weekend. I see a couple of new
          faces and a lot of returnees.

Pamela waves to Joanne and Morgan, who wave back.

                    PAMELA (CONT'D)
          So I won't keep you long because I
          know you are all anxious to see the
          wardrobe we have for the production
          number this year. Clint has put
          together the most amazing show for
          us. I am so excited.

CLINT WRIGHT stands and takes a bow. He is glam and
flamboyant. It would be impossible for another sequin to fit
on his jacket.

                    PAMELA (CONT'D)
          Plus they keep it colder than a
          meat locker in here. My gosh. My
          goose bumps have goose bumps.

The parents and contestants laugh and nod in agreement.

                    PAMELA (CONT'D)
          Okay, just a few quick points
          before we let you loose. This is a
          fun weekend. None of the stress of
          competition week but we do expect
          you to adhere to the same policies
          and code of conduct. First, pageant
          time is always on time, and by on
          time I mean fifteen minutes early.
          If we tell you to be somewhere at
          three o'clock, what time should you
          be ready?

                    AUDIENCE
          Two forty-five.

                    PAMELA
          Oh! I love it. That's right. If you
          show up at three, you are late.
          Second, girls, I know you won't
          believe this, but you can live
          without your phones. Please leave
          them in your rooms, or with your
          mom.
                    (MORE)

                    PAMELA (CONT'D)
          If you can't do that, leave them in
          your bags so you can focus on the
          tasks at hand. I do not want to see
          you Instagraming, or Twittering, or
          Shapchatting, or whatever it is
          y'all do while Clint is trying to
          teach you the numbers.

                    CONTESTANTS
          Yes, ma'am.

                    PAMELA
          Great. So, parents you will stay in
          here with me for a detailed
          explanation of what you can expect
          during competition week while the
          girls will be excused to try on
          their production outfit and then
          get their photos taken by our great
          team from BluDoor Productions. We
          love you guys! Okay, girls you are
          excused.

The contestants stand and say goodbye to their mothers.

INT. HOTEL - CONFERENCE AREA HALLWAY - CONTINUOUS

Alyssa steps into the hall where all 52 of the other
contestants have gathered. The sound of a hundred geese could
not compete with the noise of the girls talking.

Alyssa stands by herself until she sees Skyler and Maddie.
They see her and wave for her to come over.

Alyssa also sees Morgan standing with Callie and LANDON.

Landon is all legs and hair to go along with beauty, charm
and poise.

Clint steps out into the hallway, WHISTLES as loud as he can,
and once he has the girl's attention...

                    CLINT
          Girls, I know you feel like you
          haven't seen each other in years
          but that's just not the case and we
          have a million things to get done
          and half the time to do them, so I
          need you to focus on me and pay
          attention.

SERIES OF SCENES

- Clint leads the girls into another ballroom, where racks of cocktail dresses are lined along a wall. The floor has been taped off to mark the stage which they will have for state finals.

- The Contestants rush the racks of dresses to search for their size.

- Morgan exits a curtained area wearing the cocktail dress. She looks stunning.

- Alyssa exits the curtained area, looking gorgeous.

- Skyler twirls in her dress.

- Callie poses.

- Maddie models.

- Landon exits the changing booth looking like a runway model.

- A photographer's backdrop stands in one corner of the room and a husband and wife team photograph each girl in their cocktail dress.

- a group photo of all the contestants is staged. Alyssa intentionally stands next to Morgan.

- Morgan smiles at her. Alyssa is unavoidable now.

- The group photo is taken.

INT. HOTEL - BALLROOM - SAME

The contestants separate after photograph is taken. Some contestants head for the dressing area to change. Others mill around to talk (MOS).

Alyssa stops Morgan before she can leave. Morgan's hair is noticeably thinner and she looks frail.

When Alyssa grabs Morgan's arm, she can wrap her hand completely around her forearm.

                    ALYSSA
          Morgan, why have you been ignoring
          me?

                    MORGAN
          I haven't.

Alyssa just looks at her, like, "really?"

                    MORGAN (CONT'D)
          I've been super busy.

                    ALYSSA
          What happened to us all being a
          sisterhood?

                    MORGAN
          We are.

                    ALYSSA
          It sure doesn't feel like it.

                    MORGAN
          I can't help that I have stuff to
          do.

                    ALYSSA
          Look, I'm sorry for whatever I did
          to make you mad. I certainly didn't
          mean to.

                    MORGAN
          You didn't do anything.

                    ALYSSA
          Did you get my voice mail?

                    MORGAN
          Yeah. Sorry I didn't call you back,
          I --

                    ALYSSA
          Have just been really busy. I got
          it, but, Morgan, I really needed to
          talk. I could use a friend.

Morgan looks at her then at the long line of girls waiting to
change out of their cocktail dress.

                    MORGAN
          Let's talk now.

Alyssa smiles.

INT. HOTEL - CONFERENCE AREA HALLWAY - LATER

Alyssa and Morgan have found a private seating area away from
the commotion.

MORGAN
I'm really sorry your friends did
that. That sucks.

ALYSSA
Thanks. I really needed this.

MORGAN
I bet you a dozen other girls have
had the same experience.

ALYSSA
And we thought boys were the worst.

MORGAN
I'm sorry I didn't call you back. I
was a crappy friend.

ALYSSA
I'll let you make it up to me by
letting me win.

MORGAN
That seems fair.

The two laugh and hug.

Morgan pushes her hair behind her ear and a few strands come
out in her fingers. Alyssa notices.

ALYSSA
Are you okay?

MORGAN
Yeah. Of course. Why?

ALYSSA
You're super... trim.

MORGAN
My trainer has me on twice-a-days.
I swear he's the only person I ever
see.

ALYSSA
You're not dieting too?

MORGAN
No. I eat like a cow. OMG, but I'm
burning so many calories you
wouldn't know it.

KIRSTEN HAGLUND passes the girls.

                    KIRSTEN HAGLUND
          You girls better get changed.
          They're about to begin opening
          number rehearsal.

                    MORGAN
          Thank you. We totally lost track of
          time.

Morgan stands, a bit too fast, and becomes dizzy. Alyssa,
stands to steady her.

                    MORGAN (CONT'D)
          Thanks.

Kirsten watches with suspicion.

                    MORGAN (CONT'D)
          OMG! You're Kirsten Haglund. I love
          you.
               (to Alyssa)
          She was Miss America 2008.

                    KIRSTEN HAGLUND
          Are you feeling all right?

                    MORGAN
          Oh, yeah. I just stood up too fast.
          Blood must have rushed to my head
          when I realized who you were.

                    KIRSTEN HAGLUND
          Make sure you get some water and
          eat a protein bar or some almonds.

                    MORGAN
          Absolutely.

                    KIRSTEN HAGLUND
          You'd better get going. You don't
          want to be late.

                    ALYSSA
          Thank you.

Morgan and Alyssa walk away. Kirsten watches after Morgan.
Concerned.

INT. HOTEL - BALLROOM - DAY

A ballroom has been set up with circular tables for a
luncheon. The parents of the contestants are in attendance.

Camilla and Ramon sit with Joanne and Anthony at a table with other parents.

                    CAMILLA
               (to Joanne)
          So Alyssa and Morgan seemed to
          really get along.

                    JOANNE
          Yes.

Awkward pause.

                    CAMILLA
          Do you get as nervous for your
          daughter as I feel right now? I
          can't imagine doing what she's
          doing.

Camilla nervously laughs, trying desperately to break the ice with Joanne.

                    JOANNE
          No. We have done this so often it's
          like second nature now. You know I
          used to compete?

                    RAMON
          So it's like a family business.

Joanne smiles weakly. Camilla nudges Ramon under the table.

                    ANTHONY
          I like to think of it as a sports
          dynasty.

                    RAMON
          Like the Cowboys of the 80s?

                    ANTHONY
          Exactly. Joanne here is my Roger
          Staubach. My daughter is Troy
          Aikman.

                    RAMON
          Nice. That makes my daughter, Dak
          Precott.

                    ANTHONY
          Nothing wrong with that. Look what
          he did his rookie season.

                    RAMON
          Here's hoping.

Ramon and Anthony are having a great time, while the women look disgusted that their daughters are being compared to football players.

                    CAMILLA
          Can we not talk football?

                    RAMON
          Anthony and I are simply relating
          this pageant stuff to something we
          understand.

                    JOANNE
          You get used to it. I had to.

Camilla is pleased that Joanne is finally speaking to her.

                    CAMILLA
          How long did it take?

                    JOANNE
          Oh, it's a work in progress.

Anthony ignores his wife.

                    ANTHONY
          I have been trying to figure out a
          way to form a fantasy pageant
          league.

                    RAMON
          Now, you're talking.

                    CAMILLA
          You are not making a fantasy league
          of our girls.

                    ANTHONY
          I'm sorry. Not that type of
          fantasy.

                    RAMON
          We could handicap the girls based
          on local pageants and former year's
          performance.

                    ANTHONY
          We can record their gown designer
          stats and community service hours.

                    RAMON
          You'd have rookies and veterans.
          You can track how often they have
          scored in the top ten and top five.

                    ANTHONY
          We may be onto something.

                    JOANNE
          If you seriously consider doing
          this, we may be looking at a
          divorce.

                    CAMILLA
          You too buster. Let's not get
          kicked out of the organization
          before our daughter even has a
          chance to compete.

Rebuked, Ramon and Anthony turn their attention to the food
on their plates. Anthony looks over at Ramon, grins
mischievously and nods his head.

                    ANTHONY
               (mouthing words)
          We can do this.

Ramon grins.

Camilla notices and Ramon turns his smile to her. She knows.

INT. HOTEL - BALLROOM - DAY

The contestants are seated on one side of the room, while the
local and state directors, including Pamela, Paula, Tommy,
are seated in rows in front of a dance floor on the other
side of the large ballroom. Other guests include Kirsten
Haglund and WT Greer.

A few parents trickle in and sit in the back.

Tara finishes a tap routine, bows and walks off the dance
floor to sit down with the other contestants.

                    CLINT
          Next up is, Miss Allen, Alyssa
          Alvarez, singing, "They Just Keep
          Moving the Line."

Alyssa stands and walks to the center of the dance floor
where Clint has positioned a microphone stand. Alyssa wears
her talent costume, a stunning floor length gown.

The music begins and Alyssa belts out a flawless rendition of
the song.

She is pleased with herself.

So are Paula and WT. Pamela is impressed.

Morgan leads the other contestants in a rousing round of applause.

Ramon wipes a tear from his cheek as inconspicuously as possible, but Camilla notices.

Anthony, who sits nearby, gives Ramon a thumbs up. Mimes that he writes notes.

Alyssa sits down next to Morgan.

                    MORGAN
          Girl! You've been holding out on.

                    ALYSSA
          Thanks. You sure it sounded okay?

                    MORGAN
          OMG! Did Ariana Grande just enter
          the building?

Callie, leans back and taps Alyssa on the knee.

                    CALLIE
          I want to hate you right now.

                    ALYSSA
          Thanks?

                    CALLIE
          That was truly amazing. I may have
          to change my talent.

                    ALYSSA
          No. You are incredible.

                    CALLIE
          Says the girl who just slayed.

                    CLINT
          Next we have Miss Highland Park,
          Morgan Harrison, performing a
          lyrical dance.

                    MORGAN
          Wish me luck.

Morgan stands and Alyssa has to steady her.

                    ALYSSA
          I know you don't need it.

Morgan "dance walks" onto the wood floor and takes her position. She blinks repeatedly as if to clear her vision.

The music begins and Morgan begins her performance.

She is a count behind the music. She appears weak and sometimes confused.

Callie looks back and Alyssa as if to say, "what is happening?"

Morgan tries to regain her composure and continue but she struggles.

Everyone, from Clint, to Pamela to Tommy as well as Joanne and Anthony can tell something is off.

When Morgan tries a pirouette, she falls out of it and collapses.

The music stops. Tommy, Pamela and Anthony rush to attend to Morgan.

Joanne sits in her chair. Motionless. A look of disbelief quickly vanishes as she realizes other moms are looking at her. She must keep up appearances.

Kirsten Haglund kneels down beside Morgan, then looks at Pamela.

INT. HOTEL - CONFERENCE ROOM

Pamela, Tommy, Joanne, Anthony and Kirsten sit around a conference table which fills most of the space in a small conference.

>   KIRSTEN HAGLUND
>   The illness of an eating disorder
>   is not a choice nor is it a phase.

>   JOANNE
>   How can we be certain that is what
>   Morgan is dealing with? I think it
>   is simply exhaustion.

>   KIRSTEN HAGLUND
>   No offense Miss Harrison, but as
>   someone who suffered with this
>   disorder, let me tell you, your
>   daughter is in danger. Ignoring the
>   problem is not going to help.

Joanne is primed to respond but Anthony touches her hand to calm her.

                    ANTHONY
          She's right. I've worried she would
          relapse and --

                    KIRSTEN HAGLUND
          So, you have seen this behavior in
          her before?

                    ANTHONY
          Yes and we thought we had it under
          control.

                    KIRSTEN HAGLUND
          We are talking about a life-
          threatening, physical and mental
          illnesses that will require
          specialized treatment by
          professionals. My foundation can
          help you by putting you in contact
          with local specialists and help
          with any insurance issues.

                    TOMMY
          What about her competing?

                    KIRSTEN HAGLUND
          If this were my daughter I would
          want her healthy before I thought
          about any type of competition.
               (to Pamela)
          And, if this were my pageant, I
          would not want the liability of
          knowing a contestant had a serious
          disorder and I ignored the signs.

The room falls silent.

                    PAMELA
          Thank you, Kirsten. I'm glad you
          were here to consult with us. Would
          you excuse us for a moment?

Kirsten rises from the table.

                    KIRSTEN HAGLUND
          Of course. Mister and Misses
          Harrison, your daughter needs
          counseling and medical attention.
          Without both of those things, and
          the grace of God, I would not be
          standing before you today.
               (MORE)

                    KIRSTEN HAGLUND (CONT'D)
          I hope you will do what is best for
          your daughter. I will be praying
          for all of you.

Kirsten leaves.

                    PAMELA
          Well?

                    JOANNE
          Pamela, this is one woman's
          opinion. I don't think Morgan
          should be kept from competing based
          on that.

                    TOMMY
          I agree. We need a second opinion.

                    ANTHONY
          Okay, then let me be that second.
          Pamela, I agree with Kirsten. I
          believe that Morgan is suffering
          from bulimia and until it is
          treated I think she should be held
          from competition.

Another hush falls over the room.

                    PAMELA
          Competition isn't for four more
          months. Do you think she can be
          well by then?

                    TOMMY
          Most definitely.

                    JOANNE
          Yes. Of course.

                    ANTHONY
          We shall see.

INT. HOTEL ROOM - NIGHT

Alyssa knocks on the door to a hotel room.

Morgan answers.

                    ALYSSA
          Hey. Can I come in?

                    MORGAN
          Sure.

Morgan leads Alyssa into room. Morgan flops down on the bed.

                    MORGAN (CONT'D)
          I assume everyone is talking about
          this?

                    ALYSSA
          How are you feeling?

                    MORGAN
          I'm fine. I don't know why everyone
          is making such a fuss. I just
          forgot to eat lunch.

                    ALYSSA
          Morgan.

Morgan looks away.

                    MORGAN
          So what are the girls saying?

                    ALYSSA
          Who cares? What's important is that
          you get the help you need.

                    MORGAN
          My mom is angry.

                    ALYSSA
          With you?

                    MORGAN
          The organization. My dad. Everyone
          but herself. If she hadn't demanded
          perfection...

                    ALYSSA
          When I met you that first time... I
          seriously thought about quitting.

                    MORGAN
          What? Why?

                    ALYSSA
          I thought you were so beautiful. I
          thought, what am I doing here?

                    MORGAN
          C'mon?

                    ALYSSA
          Seriously. You put on that dress,
          remember?

                         MORGAN
               That's right.

                         ALYSSA
               And, I was like. Are you kidding
               me? No one can beat this girl.

                         MORGAN
               My mom will love you.

                         ALYSSA
               Morgan, I've been worried about you
               for some time. I think you know
               that.

Morgan nods.

                         MORGAN
               I'm sorry, Alyssa. I was a crappy
               friend. I didn't want you to know,
               but I knew you already did. So, I
               just decided if I ignored you then
               I didn't have to admit I was doing
               anything wrong.

                         ALYSSA
               Girl, I will not be ignored.

The two laugh.

                         MORGAN
               I realize that now. You're almost
               as bad as my mom.

Alyssa gives Morgan a look.

                         MORGAN (CONT'D)
               I said, almost.

                         ALYSSA
               Listen. I'm going to stand with you
               through this. I don't want to
               compete if you can't.

                         MORGAN
               That's silly. Why would you do
               that?

                         ALYSSA
               Because we're sisters.

INT. MORGAN'S PARENTS HOME - ENTRYWAY - DAY

The DOORBELL chimes. Joanne answers the door to find Alyssa standing on her porch. She holds up a bag of healthy breakfast food and wears a yoga outfit.

> JOANNE
> Alyssa? Hello?

> ALYSSA
> Good morning, Miss Harrison. I came to check on Morgan and help her get ready for competition.

> JOANNE
> Well, I --

Morgan comes downstairs wearing a matching yoga outfit as Alyssa.

> MORGAN
> It's okay mom. My counselor said I could do this. We're just going to go for a walk and then we will come home and I will eat.

Morgan hands Joanne the bag of food from Alyssa.

> JOANNE
> Okay.

> MORGAN
> Great. Will you keep this warm for us? See ya.

Joanne stands in the doorway, her mouth agape as Morgan and Alyssa start off for a walk.

SERIES OF SCENES

- Joanne opens the door and Alyssa stands on the porch again holding up a bag of food and carrying a yoga mat.

- Morgan and Alyssa do yoga in the back yard.

- Joanne opens the front door and lets Alyssa in without any question.

- Morgan and Alyssa sit and eat while watching a pageant video on Morgan's laptop.

- Morgan weighs herself. When she steps off the weight, Alyssa picks up the scale and walks out of the room with it.

- In the dance studio, Morgan performs her talent routine. Alyssa sits and watches. She claps when Morgan finishes.

- Alyssa sits with Morgan, Joanne and Anthony at the dinner table. The group laughs and has a good time. Morgan actually has a small second serving of food.

- Morgan helps Alyssa with her model poses and walk.

- Alyssa practices singing in front of Morgan.

INT. ALVAREZ KITCHEN - DAY

Alyssa sits with Camilla at the kitchen table. She has a spread sheet in front of her.

                    ALYSSA
          So, some I got some sponsors, and
          with Paula help I should be all
          set.

                    CAMILLA
          I told you it would work out.

                    ALYSSA
          But, I still can't afford that
          dress I really want.

                    CAMILLA
          I know, honey, but as long as you
          feel good in the dress you have --

                    ALYSSA
          I will feel better if I have the
          dress I want.

                    CAMILLA
          That's just not going to be
          possible.

Frustrated, Alyssa folds the spreadsheet.

                    ALYSSA
          Honestly, I'm not sure why I'm
          competing anymore.

                    CAMILLA
          What do you mean?

                    ALYSSA
          With Morgan healthy again, I really
          don't stand a chance. Between her
          Callie, and Landon no girl does.

                    CAMILLA
          Do you really feel that way?

                    ALYSSA
          Who am I?

                    CAMILLA
          You're a gorgeous, intelligent,
          strong woman.

                    ALYSSA
          You have to say that, you're my
          mom.

                    CAMILLA
          That doesn't make it any less true.

                    ALYSSA
          I mean, they have the best dresses,
          years of experience, not to mention
          they are gorgeous.

                    CAMILLA
          This doesn't sound like you.

                    ALYSSA
          Maybe my friends are right.

                    CAMILLA
          What friends?

                    ALYSSA
          It doesn't matter.

                    CAMILLA
          If your friends have been filling
          your head with this crap, then they
          aren't very good friends.

INT. COFFEE SHOP - DAY

A healthy and rejuvenated Morgan sits at a table with Troy.

                    TROY
          You really look great, Morgan.

                    MORGAN
          It's been a lot of work but my
          family and a good friend have been
          by my side.

                    TROY
          I've missed you.

                    MORGAN
          And yet, you haven't come by to
          visit once.

Caught like a kid with his hand in the cookie jar.

                    TROY
          You know. Classes. Stuff at the
          house.

                    MORGAN
          Sure. The important things.

                    TROY
          I'm not saying you're not
          important.

                    MORGAN
          Your actions kinda already did.
          Look, I'm not here to point out all
          your flaws -- neither of us have
          that much time --

                    TROY
          Hey--

                    MORGAN
          I just wanted to tell you to your
          face that we're done.

                    TROY
          What? Why?

                    MORGAN
          The fact that you don't know why is
          reason enough, don't you think?

                    TROY
          Wait. What?

                    MORGAN
          Don't worry about it. I know you'll
          be fine. I just wanted you to know,
          I'm stronger and wiser and for
          those reasons there simply isn't
          any time for you.

                    TROY
          I thought we loved each other?

                    MORGAN
          Love isn't toxic, Troy. And it took
          a health scare for me to realize,
          that's what you are to me. Toxic.

INT. MORGAN'S PARENTS HOME - ENTRYWAY - MORNING

Joanne opens the door to let Alyssa in.

> JOANNE
> Hi, Alyssa. Morgan's not home right
> now but may I speak with you for
> one minute?

> ALYSSA
> Of course, Mrs Harrison.

> JOANNE
> Please, I think you should call me
> Joanne now.

> ALYSSA
> Okay.

Joanne, leads Alyssa into the formal sitting room where they sit.

> ALYSSA (CONT'D)
> Is Morgan all right?

> JOANNE
> Yes. She's with her boyfriend.
> She'll be home soon. (beat) Alyssa,
> I wanted to thank you.

Alyssa starts to speak but Joanne holds up a hand to stop her.

> JOANNE (CONT'D)
> Thanks to her counselor and you,
> Morgan is well on the road to
> recovery and will be able to
> compete.

> ALYSSA
> Mostly her counselor --

> JOANNE
> She had her role, certainly, but
> Alyssa, I think you have been an
> incredible influence on Morgan.

> ALYSSA
> Thank you, Miss -- Joanne.

> JOANNE
> I mean it. Your friendship has
> meant a lot to her and...to me.

                    ALYSSA
          Well, she has been a great friend
          as well.

                    JOANNE
          I haven't seen her this happy in a
          long time.

                    ALYSSA
          You know... This competition means
          a lot to all of us, but at the end
          of the day, it doesn't mean
          everything. I mean, would I love to
          win? Yeah! But, if I don't, I have
          made some great friends, girls who
          I will be friends with for the rest
          of my life. Well you know.

                    JOANNE
          Yes. Mine were my bridesmaids.

                    ALYSSA
          Exactly. And isn't that way more
          important that who wins the crown?

Joanne contemplates Alyssa's wisdom.

Morgan enters.

                    MORGAN
          Hey! What's up?

                    JOANNE
          We were just talking about the
          pageant.

                    MORGAN
          Cool.
               (to Alyssa)
          Let's go up to my room.

Morgan exits.

Alyssa stands.

                    ALYSSA
          Thanks.

INT. MORGAN'S PARENT'S HOME - BEDROOM - DAY

Morgan is charged with excitement.

Alyssa enters, the weight of the world on her shoulders.

                    MORGAN
          So I did it!

                    ALYSSA
          Did what?

                    MORGAN
          Totally just broke up with Troy.

                    ALYSSA
          No way. Give me the four-one-one.

                    MORGAN
          I wish you could have been there.
          He was so shocked.

                    ALYSSA
          Serves him right.

                    MORGAN
          I literally won't shed a tear for
          him.

                    ALYSSA
          He doesn't deserve it.

                    MORGAN
          Seriously. I'm so glad to be rid of
          him.

                    ALYSSA
          I'm happy for you.

                    MORGAN
          You want to quiz each other on
          current events.

                    ALYSSA
          Sure.

                    MORGAN
          You sound so excited.

                    ALYSSA
          I've just got stuff on my mind.

                    MORGAN
          Want to talk about it?

                    ALYSSA
          Maybe later.

Morgan digs through her desk to find a stack of INDEX CARDS.

                    MORGAN
          You sure?

                    ALYSSA
          No. Yeah. Let's get our current
          event on.

INT. MORGAN'S PARENT'S HOME - FITNESS ROOM - LATER

Morgan and Alyssa complete a workout and sit down to rest.
They each drink from a water bottle and Morgan grabs a power
bar to eat. She offers one to Alyssa.

                    ALYSSA
          Whew. I can barely keep up with you
          anymore.

                    MORGAN
          No pain no gain.

                    ALYSSA
          I must be gaining a ton. My butt is
          killing me.

                    MORGAN
          Squats and lunges. A butt's best
          friend.

                    ALYSSA
          I don't want this type of friend.

Alyssa rubs her sore butt.

                    ALYSSA (CONT'D)
          Can I ask you something?

Joanne interrupts by popping her head into the room.

                    JOANNE
          I'm going to Juice Bar. You all
          want anything?

                    MORGAN
          I'll take an acai bowl.

                    ALYSSA
          Nothing for me thanks.

                    JOANNE
          You sure?

                    ALYSSA
          Thank you. I have to go in a minute
          anyway.

                    JOANNE
          Okay.

Joanne exits.

                    MORGAN
          What's up? You've seemed kind of
          distracted today.

                    ALYSSA
          Yeah. (beat) Do you ever have any
          doubts when you compete?

Morgan laughs.

                    MORGAN
          You have to ask?

                    ALYSSA
          No. That was dumb.

                    MORGAN
          What's going on?

                    ALYSSA
          I don't know. Lately, I just don't
          feel like I belong in the
          competition. Like I'm an imposter
          and if I go on stage everyone wil
          know.

                    MORGAN
          For starters, you're my biggest
          competition --

                    ALYSSA
          Yeah, right.

                    MORGAN
          Seriously.

                    ALYSSA
          I think Callie and Landon may
          disagree.

                    MORGAN
          Callie and I have been trading
          titles for years. Landon will be in
          the top five for sure. But you.
          You're the dark horse.

                    ALYSSA
          You think?

                    MORGAN
          I know. Ever since spring meeting
          there's been talk.

                    ALYSSA
          Really.

                    MORGAN
          I don't know who said what to get
          in your head, but stop it.

                    ALYSSA
          Easy for you --

                    MORGAN
          Yeah. Ha. Hard to come back at
          someone who is living it.

Alyssa laughs.

                    MORGAN (CONT'D)
          I've learned something from my
          counselor. You have to love
          yourself more than you allow others
          to dictate how you feel.

Alyssa nods.

                    MORGAN (CONT'D)
          Honestly, we're not competing with
          anyone but ourselves.

                    ALYSSA
          Thanks.

                    MORGAN
          I know you have our faith. Did you
          ever stop to think, maybe you were
          placed in this position, and this
          is your time?

EXT. HOTEL - DAY

Cars fill the porte-cochère of the hotel as contestants and
their parents overload bell-carts with dresses, suitcases,
make-up kits, pillows and more.

Valets scramble to keep track of car keys and cars, bell men
try to keep carts from tipping over. It is mass mayhem of
model-perfect girls.

INT. HOTEL - CONFERENCE AREA HALLWAY - SAME

Contestants and their parents queue to register with the state competition board and get their tickets for all of the week's events.

A line of lovely ladies, snakes through the conference hall lobby. The energy level is so high it could power downtown Dallas.

Parents sort through paperwork and turn in paperwork.

Alyssa and Camilla enter through the conference hall entrance.

Alyssa looks around the sea of pageant contestants looking for Morgan. She sees Maddie and waves.

Joanne approaches. She hugs Alyssa and Camilla.

                    JOANNE
          Here we go!

                    ALYSSA
          I can't believe it's finally here!

                    CAMILLA
          My nerves are already on edge.

                    JOANNE
          Just wait. But, there is a good bar
          in the hotel.

Joanne winks.

                    JOANNE (CONT'D)
          Have you checked in yet?

                    ALYSSA
          Not yet.

                    JOANNE
          If you need any help, let me know.
          It can be a bit overwhelming the
          first time.

                    CAMILLA
          Thank you.

                    JOANNE
          I was able to request that you and
          Morgan room together.

                    CAMILLA
          That's great.

                    ALYSSA
          I thought it was random?

                    JOANNE
          Sometimes it pays to stick around
          for a few decades. Plus under the
          circumstances...

                    PAGEANT MOM (O.C.)
          Joanne!

Joanne looks up to see a familiar face.

                    JOANNE
          Got to run.
               (to Camilla)
          Anthony and I bought tickets for
          you and Ramon to sit next to us
          during the pageant. I hope that's
          all right?

                    CAMILLA
          Sure.

                    JOANNE
          Great. I'll talk with later. So
          much to get done.

Joanne rushes away.

Camilla looks at Alyssa.

Paula approaches. She is all smiles.

                    PAULA
          Great. You're here. I was about to
          call you.

                    ALYSSA
          Just got here. This is a lot to
          process.

                    PAULA
          That's for sure. But, it runs like
          a well oiled machine. Where's
          Ramon?

Camilla points outside.

EXT. HOTEL - SAME

Ramon unloads the car with all of Alyssa's costumes, gowns
and stuff. Everything she will need this week.

INT. HOTEL - CONFERENCE AREA HALLWAY - SAME

Paula hugs Alyssa and then Camilla.

                    PAULA
          Listen. You are totally ready for
          this. Drink this in. It's a
          wonderful experience. Most of all,
          have fun.

Morgan approaches. She carries a garment bag.

                    MORGAN
          There you are!

Morgan gives Alyssa the biggest hug.

                    PAULA
          Camilla, do you have Alyssa's
          packet?

                    CAMILLA
          All ready.

Camilla holds up a stuffed manila envelope.

                    PAULA
          Let me help you get her signed in.

Paula and Camilla walk over to the sign in table.

Morgan hands Alyssa the garment bag.

                    ALYSSA
          What this?

                    MORGAN
          Open it.

Alyssa unzips the bag to reveal the beautiful emerald dress
she wanted at the boutique.

                    ALYSSA
          No! This is amazing. I can't --

                    MORGAN
          You can't refuse. I know. I'm
          pretty sure it should fit, but just
          in case, there's a seamstress in
          the hotel here for girls who need
          last minute alterations.

                    ALYSSA
          Oh. My. God. I can't believe this.

                    MORGAN
          I told you -- (whispering) I only
          want to win against my biggest
          competition.

INT. THEATER STAGE - DAY

Opening number production rehearsal. Clint leads the girls
through the dance moves.

Morgan and Alyssa are each positioned near the front of the
stage.

All of the contestants are wearing the cocktail dresses that
they tried on at the spring meeting.

INT. HOTEL - CONFERENCE ROOM

Morgan enters the conference room where the JUDGES are seated
behind a table. Morgan takes her place behind a podium across
from the judges.

                    MORGAN
          Good afternoon ladies and
          gentlemen, my name is Morgan
          Harrison, Miss Highland Park.

                    JUDGE 1
          Morgan, social media can be used
          both for positive and negative
          reasons. How can we make it so it
          is mostly used for good?

                    MORGAN
          Great question.

INT. HOTEL - CONFERENCE ROOM

Alyssa enters the conference room where the Judges are seated
behind a table. She takes her place behind a podium across
from the judges.

                    ALYSSA
          Hello. My name is Alyssa Alvarez,
          Miss Allen.

                    JUDGE 2
          Alyssa, your platform is about
          promoting mental health, how do you
          actually carry out that message?

                    ALYSSA
          Thank you for your question. You
          know recently I was faced with
          helping a close friend deal with a
          disorder which is as much mental as
          well as physical.

INT. THEATER STAGE

It is preliminary competition.

SERIES OF SCENES

- The contestants perform the opening production number they
were rehearsing earlier.

- After the number, the contestants rush off stage and there
is a flurry of activity as some change into swimsuits and
others into even gowns.

- Morgan, Alyssa, Maddie, Callie, Skyler, and Landon walk
across stage in their fitness swimwear.

Morgan looks healthy and vibrant.

Alyssa looks confident and relaxed.

- Joanne, Anthony, Camilla, and Ramon sit together in the
audience cheering.

Joanne and Anthony hold up large signs with pictures of
Morgan.

- The contestants gracefully walk out on stage, grouped
together in a parade of colors, each wearing stunning evening
gowns. It is a venerable rainbow of colors and dress styles.

- Callie sings her talent song. She is strong.

- More backstage craziness, as the contestants rush about
getting ready for the various portions of the show that they
are a part of.

- Skyler stands on stage next to a FORMER STATE TITLE HOLDER
who holds a piece of paper with the on-stage question.

                    FORMER STATE TITLE HOLDER
          Your question is from Judge number
          two. Recently political correctness
          has us changing school and street
          names away from Confederate
          figures. Now protestors are turning
          their attention to Columbus and
          other early explorers who, they say
          stole land from Native Americans.
          Do you think this is right, or
          wrong, and why?

                    SKYLER
          I do understand why some historical
          figures could offend people because
          of what they stood for, but the
          fact is, these people were a part
          of our history and that cannot be
          ignored. For good or evil, these
          people made contributions that
          shaped this country. Should all of
          them be celebrated with statues?
          No, I do not believe so, but, I
          would ask, once we start changing
          our history, where do we stop?
          Thank you.

The audience applauds as Skyler poses then walks off stage.

INT. THEATER LOBBY - EVENING

A crowd of well dressed directors, parents, family and
friends stand in groups talking (MOS). A nervous kenetic,
energy fills the room. People hold signs supporting their
contestants and flowers.

Camilla and Ramon stand with Paula.

                    PAULA
          She really did great this week. We
          couldn't have hoped for better.

                    RAMON
          So, what do you think her chances
          are?

                    PAULA
          I don't want to say anything.
               (whispers)
          But, damn good.

They all smile.

                    RAMON
          Good. That's good.

                    CAMILLA
          Is someone starting to get into
          this a little?

Yasmine and Kristi approach.

Camilla is surprised to see them.

                    CAMILLA (CONT'D)
          Hello girls. I didn't know you were
          coming.

                    KRISTI
          We wanted to surprise Alyssa.

                    CAMILLA
          I'm sure she will be thrilled.

                    ANNOUNCER (O.S.)
          Ladies and gentlemen, the final
          night of competition will begin in
          ten minutes. We ask that you take
          your seats.

                    PAULA
          This is it!

INT. THEATER STAGE - OFF STAGE - NIGHT

Morgan and Alyssa stand side by side, holding hands behind
the curtain to the theater.

                    MORGAN
          Whatever happens tonight, you'll
          always be my sister.

                    ALYSSA
          I'm going to hold you to that.

The music begins. The lights go on. The curtains open.

INT. THEATER STAGE - CONTINUOUS

The 50 contestants parade across the stage in their cocktail
dresses for opening number.

Each contestant walks to the front of the stage, where three microphones are positioned.

> MORGAN
> I'm Miss Highland Park, Morgan Harrison.

> MADDIE
> I'm Miss Tyler, Maddie Ferguson.

> SKYLER
> My name is Sklyer West, your Miss Fort Worth.

> CALLIE
> I'm Callie Parker, Miss Fairview.

> LANDON
> I'm Miss Houston, Landon Hope.

> ALYSSA
> I'm Alyssa Alvarez, Miss Allen.

INT. THEATER STAGE - LATER

Moments later, all of the contestants stand at attention as the show's EMCEE walks across the stage to receive the envelope with the Top 12 contestant's names.

> EMCEE
> It's the time we have all been waiting for. After a long week of competition, girls, are you ready to find out who is moving on to compete tonight for the title of Miss Texas?

The girls applaud politely while the crowd cheers enthusiastically.

ANGLE ON AUDIENCE

Joanne cheers and whistles. Anthony waves a sign with Morgan's picture on it.

Camilla and Ramon wave colorful light wands and cheer.

ANGLE ON MORGAN

Morgan smiles. This is old hat to her but she still gets a buzz from it.

ANGLE ON ALYSSA

Deep breaths. Big smile. She can do this.

ANGLE ON KRISTI AND YASMINE

The two girls clap enthusiastically. Kristi SCREAMS.

ANGLE ON THE EMCEE

Back at her podium on the edge of the stage, the Emcee looks
at the list of names.

> EMCEE (CONT'D)
> All right. Here we go. The names of
> the top ten contestants who will go
> on to compete in all areas of
> competition again tonight are, in
> random order...

Long, dramatic pause

> EMCEE (CONT'D)
> Miss Fairview!

The crowd cheers. Callie walks to a designated spot on the
stage. She smiles and waves to the audience and thanks the
judges.

> EMCEE (CONT'D)
> Next is, Miss Houston!

A large section of the audience cheers as Landon walks to a
mark on the stage. She smiles to the judges and her cheering
section.

> EMCEE (CONT'D)
> Our third contestant moving on is,
> Miss Highland Park!

Morgan walks forward.

ANGLE ON AUDIENCE

Joanne and Anthony stand and scream. Waving to Morgan.

ANGLE ON STAGE

> EMCEE (CONT'D)
> Come on down, Miss Tyler! (beat)
> Our next contestant is, Miss
> Lubbock! (beat) We are half way
> through the list. Next, let's
> welcome, Miss Fort Worth! (beat)

After each name the contestants walks to a MARK on the stage next to the previous contestant. They hug each other then smile at audience.

ANGLE ON ALYSSA

Alyssa rubs the palms of her hands on her dress to dry them. She works to keep a smile on her face as more names are called and none of them are her's.

> EMCEE (O.S.) (CONT'D)
> Take your place, Miss Dallas!

Alyssa claps politely as she watches another girl walk to the front of the stage. *She wishes it was her.*

ANGLE ON STAGE

The seven contestants whose names have been called line up across the stage. They beam with excitement.

> EMCEE (CONT'D)
> Only three spots left. Taking one
> of those spots is, Miss Allen!

Alyssa stands perfectly still. She can't believe her name was called.

ANGLE ON AUDIENCE

Camilla screams with joy and jumps up and down. Ramon is shocked but proud and excited.

Anthony congratulates Ramon. Joanne hugs Camilla.

ANGLE ON STAGE

Morgan motions for Alyssa to move forward. Tara nudges Alyssa.

                              TARA
                    Go ahead!

Still in shock, Alyssa walks forward.

                              EMCEE
                    Here we go, the last two names...

Alyssa takes her rightful place near the front of the stage.
The bright lights blur her vision but she can see her parents
waving. She raises the sign language, "I love you" to her
parents in the audience.

Morgan looks down the line to Alyssa, smiles and winks.

The reading of the last two names is inconsequential at this
point.

INT. THEATER - BACKSTAGE

Morgan greets Alyssa backstage.

                              MORGAN
                    I told you.

                              ALYSSA
                    I can't believe it.

Clint rushes by.

                              CLINT
                    No time for chit-chat, girls. Let's
                    go!

INT. THEATER STAGE - LATER

Morgan performs her talent dance. The music, lights, costume,
everything is perfect.

She performs a flawless routine.

Alyssa watches from the side of the stage and is as proud as
anyone in the audience, including Joanne.

Morgan completes her routine, bows and runs off stage and
straight into Alyssa's arms. They hug.

                              ALYSSA
                    That was seriously, the most
                    beautiful thing I have ever seen.

                    MORGAN
          Let's hope the judges think it's as
          beautiful as your singing.

INT. THEATER STAGE - LATER

The lights are down and Alyssa walks to center stage where a
single microphone stand, waits for her.

The music begins and a spotlight cuts through the theater to
illuminate Alyssa.

She sings.

When she finishes the audience stands to their feet.

INT. THEATER - BACKSTAGE

Alyssa exits the stage and into the arms of Morgan.

                    MORGAN
          You just had to bring down the
          house, didn't you?

Alyssa is near tears. Tears of joy.

Callie passes by.

                    CALLIE
          I've been singing a long time, but
          I have never commanded the stage
          like that.

                    ALYSSA
          Thank you.

                    MORGAN
          We've got ourselves a Cinderella
          story, tonight.

Callie smiles and walks away.

                    ALYSSA
          Tonight is like a dream.

                    MORGAN
          Well don't wake up yet. We've got
          one more round to go.

                    ALYSSA
          Oh God. On stage question. But
          that's only for top five.

                         MORGAN
              Girl, do you think after a
              performance like that, you won't be
              in top five? Please.

                         ALYSSA
              I don't know. Everyone is so
              talented.

                         MORGAN
              Sure we are, but you just took it
              to another level. (beat) You know,
              without this organization, and
              without you, I literally would not
              be alive.

                         ALYSSA
              You're being dramatic.

                         MORGAN
              I'm serious. I never told you all
              what my doctor said. I owe you a
              lot, Alyssa. Thank you.

The two being to cry.

                         ALYSSA
              Is this your plot to win? Make me
              cry and ruin my make up?

Tears turn to laughter.

                         ALYSSA (CONT'D)
              I want to thank you too?

                         MORGAN
              For what?

                         ALYSSA
              For making me feel like I should be
              here.

INT. THEATER STAGE - LATER

A SINGER performs the song "Invincible" (if possible) by
Kelly Clarkson. The music continues for the final scenes.

INT. THEATER STAGE

Five contestants, among them, Landon, Callie, Morgan, Maddie,
and Alyssa, stand on stage in their evening gowns. They hold
each other's hands.

Alyssa is wearing the stunning emerald dress. She radiates on stage.

>   EMCEE
>   We've come to the final portion of
>   our competition. Each contestant
>   will be asked one question from our
>   judges and will have ninety seconds
>   to answer. First up is my Miss
>   Houston!

While, Landon walks across the stage, Morgan squeezes Alyssa's hand. The two look at each other and smile.

Alyssa looks out over the sea of faces in the audience. She drinks in the entire view. *How many girls have stood in this spot?*

Alyssa sees Camilla wave to her and she smiles and nods her head without being obvious.

The Emcee's voice brings her back to the present.

>   EMCEE (CONT'D)
>   Next is Miss Allen.

Alyssa gracefully walks to the other side of the stage where a FORMER TITLE HOLDER stands with a bowl filled with folded paper.

The Former Title Holder motions for Alyssa to take a sheet out of the bowl.

Alyssa does and hands it to the Former Title Holder.

>   FORMER STATE TITLE HOLDER
>   Your question comes from judge
>   number five. What experience in
>   your life would you trade, or
>   repeat, and why?

>   ALYSSA
>   That's easy. Honestly, I would
>   repeat my entire time competing in
>   the pageants of this organization.
>   This time I would trust that I was
>   supposed to be here and not listen
>   to negative voices that would try
>   to discourage me. My time in this
>   organization has been some of the
>   most confidence boosting,
>   empowering and rewarding moments of
>   my life.
>   (MORE)

>   ALYSSA (CONT'D)
>   I know I have made life long
>   friends, and I truly feel I have
>   fulfilled a great calling on my
>   life by being here. Thank you.

Alyssa acknowledges the judges, smiles and returns to her mark across the stage, next to Morgan.

Morgan smiles and winks at Alyssa.

ANGLE ON AUDIENCE

Yasmine and Kristi sit in the audience. They courtesy applaud but realize they were the target of Alyssa's words.

INT. THEATER STAGE - LATER

The top five contestants stand at center stage. The other 45 contestants stand as a backdrop for them.

The Former Miss Texas and Clint stand nearby holding crown, sash and flowers.

>   EMCEE
>   The competition is complete. We are
>   just waiting for the scores from
>   our judges to be tabulated. While
>   we wait, I'll tell you a quick
>   joke. They teach us these in host
>   school. A man walks into a bar
>   where a cat is sitting in a chair
>   playing poker. He asks the
>   bartender, "Is that cat really
>   playing poker?" The bartender says,
>   "Yeah, but he's not very good.
>   Whenever he has a hot hand, he
>   starts wagging his tail."

The audience groans.

>   EMCEE (CONT'D)
>   I said I would tell you a joke. I
>   didn't say it would be a good one.
>   Okay, it looks like the auditors
>   are ready. Are you ready audience?

Loud cheers.

The Emcee walks across the stage to get the final scores then back to her podium.

                    EMCEE (CONT'D)
          I've always thought it would be
          easier if they brought the scores
          to me. Do you know how hard it is
          to walk in a dress like this? Isn't
          this a beautiful dress though? It
          was provided by Terry Costa
          Boutique, where all of my gowns
          tonight are from. Thank you Terry
          Costa for making me look
          incredible. Okay, let's get to the
          winners.

The Emcee looks at the card, then out at the audience.

                    EMCEE (CONT'D)
          Okay, our fourth runner up is, Miss
          Tyler.

Clint hands Maddie a large bouquet of flowers and ushers her
to the side.

                    EMCEE (CONT'D)
          The third runner up is, Miss
          Fairview.

Callie, accepts the flowers and moves to the side.

                    EMCEE (CONT'D)
          Our second runner up is, Miss
          Houston.

Only Morgan and Alyssa are left standing at center stage.
They turn to face each other while the audience screams and
cheers like it was the super bowl of beauty.

ANGLE ON THE AUDIENCE

Joanne and Camilla are both crying and holding each other's
hands just as their daughters are on stage.

Anthony claps Ramon on the shoulders.

BACK ON STAGE

Morgan smiles at Alyssa.

                    MORGAN
          You got this, sis!

                         EMCEE
          I will now announce the next Miss
          Texas, which means the other
          contestant will be the first runner
          up and perform the duties of Miss
          Texas in the event the winner
          cannot. Ladies and gentleman, our
          next Miss Texas is --

                                        FADE TO BLACK.

DURING CREDITS

Photo of Alyssa in shock.

Photo of Alyssa being crowned.

Photo of Alyssa walking the stage as the new Miss Texas.

Photo of Alyssa being hugged by Morgan.

Photo of Alyssa being hugged by all the contestants.

Photo of Alyssa posed with the Top Five.

Photo of Alyssa asleep on bed wearing crown and sash.

www.ingramcontent.com/pod-product-compliance
Lightning Source LLC
Chambersburg PA
CBHW062059090426
42741CB00015B/3282

9 781735 008325